三民叢書

規範邏輯導論

何 秀 煌 著

1970

三 民 書 局 印 行

內政部出版登記證內版臺業字第六六〇號

中華民國五十九年十一月初版

規範邏輯導論 調整基本定價伍元

精裝定價新台幣 壹佰元
美金 二元五角 (US$2.5)

著作者　何　秀　煌

出版者　三民書局有限公司

發行所　三民書局有限公司
　　　　臺北市重慶南路一段七十七號

印刷所　中　臺　印　刷　廠
　　　　臺中市公園路三十七號

規範邏輯導論

何秀煌 著

1970

三民書局出版

DEONTIC LOGIC AND IMPERATIVE LOGIC

DEONTIC LOGIC
AND
IMPERATIVE LOGIC

by

HSIU-HWANG HO

Assistant Professor of Philosophy
Stanislaus State College

SAN MIN BOOK CO., LTD.
Taipei, Taiwan, China
1970

San Min Book Co., Ltd.
Taipei, Taiwan

To the memory of

PROFESSOR HENRY S. LEONARD

PREFACE

This monograph deals with the problem of whether current systems of deontic and imperative logic formalize satisfactorily our intuitive deontic and imperative notions, and the problem of whether those systems can be used to justify normative reasonings. Some semantical inadequacies of the current systems are noted and suggestions are made for their removal.

Chapter One contains reconstructions of certain well-known systems of deontic logic: von Wright's system vW, Fisher-Åqvist's system FÅ, a family of systems called OT*, OS4* and OS5*, and Anderson's systems OM, OM' and OM." The systems OT*, OS4* and OS5* are developed quite thoroughly: a number of important theorems are proved, the problem of irreducible deontic modalities is solved for each system and containment relations among the systems are studied. Certain familiar problems and difficulties of current deontic logic are examined, for instance, the paradoxes of "derived obligation", contrary-to-duty imperatives and Chisholm's dilemma, the Kantian Principle and the paradox of the Good Samaritan.

In Chapter Two certain amendments are made to the systems OT*, OS4* and OS5*. The deontic operator 'O' (obligation) is explained in terms of, and hence relativized to, a set of moral rules. Deontic variables are taken to range over propositions that we call *circumstantialized act-propositions*, or simply CM-act-propositions, in which the elements of agent, time and location of endeavoring are specified. An attempt is made to justify these amendments by metaethical observations. Hintikka-style semantics is furnished. Quantifiers are readily introducible into the amended systems, and it is argued that quantified deontic logic is necessary to express some moral codes or moral principles. Some suggestions about solving in the amended systems the paradoxes and difficulties listed above are advanced. Finally, the problem of introducing alethic modalities into deontic logic is raised. The Kantian Principle and the "law" that what is necessary is obligatory and what is impossible is forbidden are discussed.

In the last chapter the relation between the evaluative and directive uses of language in a moral context is examined. An attempt is made to show that a deontic logic and the corresponding imperative logic are isomorphic models of a related normative logic. An attempt is also made to explicate the notion of normative validity. A partial characterization of the truth conditions for deontic (or imperative) sentences is proposed, and it is argued that the usual definition of (assertoric) validity is applicable to normative arguments. Finally, the problem of the possibility of imperative logic is raised. Jørgensen's dilemma and related problems are examined. Two un- orthodox imperative operators, which are imperative counter- parts of 'You are permitted to do...' and 'It is indifferent that you do...', are introduced. Attention to these operators seems to contribute to a correct understanding of certain disputed argument forms.

Three appendices are included: a list of axioms and rules, a list of definitions, and a list of theorems. There is also a comprehensive bibliography that lists most of the important works in deontic and imperative logic through 1968.

The author wishes to express his deep gratitude to Professor Gerald J. Massey for his untiring and time-consuming careful reading of the material when it was submitted as the author's doctoral dissertation to Michigan State University in 1969. Professor Massey's detailed criticism and helpful suggestions have led to many improvements both in formulation and in argumentation.

Thanks are also due to Professor Herbert E. Hendry and Professor George C. Kerner with whom discussions always turned out to be fruitful and beneficial to the author.

TABLE OF CONTENTS

4

§ 1. INTRODUCTION

The behavior of deontic predicates such as 'obligatory', 'permissible' and 'forbidden' has long been receiving philosophers' attention. As early as in the Middle Ages, it was observed that there exists a similarity between the concept obligation and the concept necessity on the one hand, and the behavior of the concept permission and of the concept possibility on the other. However, the philosophical treatment of these deontic concepts had been largely peripheral and made in passing until early this century when Ernst Mally tried to formalize systematically the deontic concepts.[1] It was he who first used the word 'deontik' and called his study of these concepts 'Deontik Logik'.

Subsequently, a remarkable number of efforts have been made either directly in deontic logic or in fields closely related to it, e. g., in the logic of imperatives or in the logic of commands. Examples of these efforts made before 1950 can be found most significantly in the following literature: Kurt Grelling [1939], Karel Reach [1939], Karl Menger [1939], Albert Hofstadter and John Charles Chinoweth McKinsey [1939], Alf Ross [1941] and Herbert Gaylord Bohnert [1945].

It is perhaps sound to say, however, that the ice of

---

1 See Mally [1926]. The author-*cum*-date reference is made to the bibliography at the end of this book.

modern deontic study was not really broken until the late 1950's when the Finnish logician Georg Henrik von Wright published his earliest studies in deontic logic with an effort to formalize the deontic concepts of permission, obligation, prohibition and commitment.[2] Since the publication of the earliest papers by von Wright, the study of deontic concepts has received widespread philosophical attention both in the English-speaking world and in Scandinavian countries.[3]

Although hardly twenty years have elapsed, we find a wide range of deontic logics on display. Among them some systems are based upon standard propositional logic,[4] others take alethic modal logics as their cornerstones.[5] There are still others in which quantifiers play an indispensable role.[6] Besides, of all the varieties some systems are two-valued,[7] others three-valued;[8] some systems formalize the relativized deontic concepts,[9] others incorporate tense-logical notions as their basic concepts.[10] Furthermore, some philosophers discuss deontic logic in the context of, or in coordination with, imperative logic or directive logic;[11] others base their deontic logics on another formalized or formalizable system,

2 In English, the word 'deontic' was coined, according to von Wright, by Charles Dunbar Broad. See von Wright [1951a].

3 See, especially, von Wright [1951a] and [1951b].

4 For example, von Wright [1951a], [1951b], [1956], [1965a] and Fisher [1961b].

5 E. g., Anderson [1956] and Prior [1957].

6 See Hintikka [1957].

7 Von Wright [1951b].

8 Fisher [1961b] and Åqvist [1963b].

9 Von Wright [1956] and Rescher [1958].

10 Von Wright [1965b] and Åqvist [1966]. cf. §14.

11 E. g., Geach[1958], Castañeda [1958], [1968], and Ross [1968].

such as the "logic of better",[12] and so on. This list of variety in deontic logic can be extended considerably, and all of the deontic systems are devised to capture the formal structure of deontic concepts.

In the course of development of these various deontic systems, different types of procedure to single out the "deontic truths" have also been advanced. Among them, axiomatics is hardly a new technique as one may expect. The truth table or matrix method and the [normal form method are also commonly used. In addition, Quine's truth-value analysis, Hintikka's model-set method, Kripkean model structure together with Beth's semantical tableaux, and Fitch's subordinate proof, all have found their ways into deontic logic.

This brief description of deontic logic may lead one to conclude that the modern development of deontic logic has now reached a mature and advanced stage. This conclusion, however, is too hasty if not totally unjustifiable. For one thing, logic may not be just a game of manipulating symbols. We usually intend a logic to be a formalization or systematization of a set of concepts of which the under-lying "logic" is intuitively conceived. In our present case, this set of concepts is the so-called deontic concepts: obligation, permission, prohibition (forbiddance) and com-mitment. A deontic logic is meant to explicate these concepts. Hence, the success of a deontic logician depends not only on whether he has a syntactically well-built system, but also on whether his system admits of a sound [semantical interpretation which is genuinely deontic. From this point of

12 Åqvist [1963c].

view, it is not without good reason that some philosophers also call deontic logic the *logic of obligation*. This reminds us from the very beginning what deontic logic aims at, and provides us with an intuitive ground to justify its degree of success.

It is a common belief, and a usual practice, too, among deontic logicians that the concepts of obligation, permission and prohibition are interdefinable with the help of some logical constants (e. g., the negation and conjunction connectives).[13] It follows immediately that the logic of obligation, the logic of permission, and the logic of prohibition are, or could be, one and the same logic. But what about the logic of commitment? Is the concept "commitment" definable in terms of one or several of the other deontic concepts with perhaps the help of certain logical constants? The answer is far less definite.

Von Wright first tried to formalize the concept of commitment in terms of obligation and the material conditional.[14] Since that proposal was put forward, criticism and new proposals have been mounting in the literature. But until now there seems to be no single satisfactory formulation which is commonly accepted by deontic logicians. To make the situation even worse, Roderick M. Chisholm introduced the so-called contrary-to-duty imperative into deontic studies,[15] thereby adding to the already puzzling problem a new dimension of difficulty.

This is just an indication of the semantic difficulties which a deontic logician encounters. In addition, the problems

13 See, for example (D2. 1) — (D2. 3) in next section.
14 Von Wright [1951a].
15 Chisholm [1963a].

of deontic logic come from pragmatic considerations, too. Some philosophers tend to think that a sound deontic system should be able to function as a logic of imperative (or directive) inference which can be used to justify imperative reasoning just as ordinary logic has been used to justify descriptive or assertoric reasoning. Indeed, some philosophers, notably Ross [1968], even call a logic of imperatives deontic logic. And the problems of imperative logic have often been treated as the problems of deontic logic.

There are, then, two classes of problems we have so far mentioned. On the one hand, there are semantic problems of how to interpret a deontic logic as a sound logic of obligation and other deontic concepts. Or, what turns out to be the same thing, the problem of how to "correctly" formalize our intuitive deontic concepts. And, on the other hand, we have the pragmatic problems of how our logic can be used as a logic of imperatives. These are, indeed, two sets of problems we want to consider in this discussion.

But before we set out to discuss these problems, we shall first try to present some systems of deontic logic. We shall treat three systems OT*, OS4* and OS5* quite thoroughly, and compare them with von Wright's system vW, Fisher and Åqvist's system FÅ and Anderson's systems OM, OM' and OM''. This will help us to locate our problems precisely in their proper contexts, and make us understand more adequately the nature of the problems.

CHAPTER ONE

SOME DEONTIC SYSTEMS

§2. VON WRIGHT'S SYSTEM VW

G. H. von Wright may be properly thought of as a pioneer in the modern study of deontic logic. His early works in the 1950's have been the principal sources of inspiration and guidance in the development of deontic logic. It was mainly from his works that current systems of deontic logic sprang and received their present shapes. Moreover, during these past seventeen years (1951—1968), deontic logicians or deontically minded philosophers have been greatly indebted to his constant introduction of original ideas and his steady contribution of new results. For instance, his idea of relativizing deontic concepts, in particular, the concept of relative or conditional permission, led to the development of the system of conditional permission.[1] And his introduction of a special type of tense-logical connectives gave rise to another type of deontic logic, namely tense-deontic logic.[2]

In order to appreciate the problems of deontic logic mentioned in the last section, let us first of all reconstruct the earliest system of modern deontic logic proposed by von Wright in 1951, namely, his system of the *logic of permission*.[3]

---

1 See von Wright [1956], [1964] and Rescher [1958], [1962].
2 Von Wright [1965b], [1966] and Åqvist [1966]. See §14.
3 For the sake of uniformity in our discussion, we do not try to be in strict conformity with von Wright's original symbolism and formulation.

System vW has the following vocabulary and forma-tion rules:

I. Vocabulary

i) Individual variables: 'a', 'b', 'c', 'a_1', 'b_1', 'c_1', 'a_2',... These variables range over act-types or "act-qualifying properties".

ii) Deontic connectives: '$\sim$', '&', 'v', '$\supset$', '$\equiv$'[4]

iii) Deontic predicate: 'P' (which may be read as "It is permissible that…").

iv) Sentential connectives: '$\sim$'. '&', 'v', '$\supset$', '$\equiv$'[4] (with the usual semantics).

v) Grouping indicators: '[',']'

II. Formation rules

i) An individual variable standing alone is a (deontic) *name* (an atomic name).[5]

ii) If α and β are (deontic) names, then $\ulcorner\sim\alpha\urcorner$, $\ulcorner[\alpha\ \&\ \beta]\urcorner$, $\ulcorner[\alpha v\beta]\urcorner$, $\ulcorner[\alpha\supset\beta]\urcorner$ and $\ulcorner[\alpha\equiv\beta]\urcorner$ are (deontic) names (molecular names).

iii) If α is a name, than $\ulcorner P\alpha\urcorner$ is a sentence (an atomic sentence). We call it a *P-sentence*.[5]

iv) If A and B are sentences, then $\ulcorner\sim A\urcorner$, $\ulcorner[A\&B]\urcorner$, $\ulcorner[AvB]\urcorner$, $\ulcorner[A\supset B]\urcorner$ and $\ulcorner[A\equiv B]\urcorner$ are sentences (mole-cular sentences).

v) Only those formulas which can be formed by i) and ii) are names, and only those formulas which can be

---

4 The same set of symbols are used both as deontic connectives and as sentential connectives. But these two classes of objects can always be effectively distinguished one from the other by the formation rules. Hence, this ambiguity is superficial and harmless.

5 Von Wright uses 'name' and 'sentence' in [1951a], some logician may prefer to use 'term' and 'well-formed formula', respectively.

formed by iii) and iv) are sentences.

The concepts of obligation, forbiddance and (moral) indifference can, then, be defined in terms of the concept of permission in the following way:

(D2. 1) $\ulcorner O\alpha \urcorner =_{Df} \ulcorner \sim P \sim \alpha \urcorner$

(D2. 2) $\ulcorner F\alpha \urcorner =_{Df} \ulcorner \sim P\alpha \urcorner$

(D2. 3) $\ulcorner I\alpha \urcorner =_{Df} \ulcorner [P\alpha \ \& \ P \sim \alpha] \urcorner$

$\ulcorner O\alpha \urcorner$, $\ulcorner F\alpha \urcorner$ and $\ulcorner I\alpha \urcorner$ may be called, respectively, an O-sentence, an F-sentence, and an I-sentence.

Von Wright, then, asks the question: What are the "things" which are pronounced obligatory, permissible, forbidden, etc.? The answer, according to him, is straight-forward, namely, "acts", or more precisely speaking, act-qualifying properties. However, it should be pointed out that the concept of an act (or act-type) is difficult to define. Actually in von Wright's earliest writings, the meaning of that term is not precisely construed. For instance, we may ask the following question: Is there any difference between saying that *act a* is permissible and the *performance* of act *a* is permissible? Some people may be inclined to say no, having in mind that to say "the performance of act *a*" is just a redundant way of saying "act *a*", because the very concept of act implies the concept of performance. It seems that von Wright himself shares this view, for we find that he speaks indiscriminately of an act and the performance of an act. For example, in [1951a] he uses, among other things, the following expressions:

(2. 1) If an act is obligatory,...

(2. 2) If doing what we ought to do commits us to...

(2. 3) If failure to perform an act commits us to... [6]

Thus in our reproduction of his system vW, we are going to interpret the individual variables in the same manner. We will read 'Pa' either as "a is permissible" or as "the performance of a is permissible", and leave open, for the time being, the question of how we should properly analyze a deontic sentence.

Let us then agree with von Wright in saying that an act is either performed or not performed. This is called the *performance value* of an act. If we let '1' and '0' denote the performance values "performance" and "non-performance", respectively, and let 'f' denote the *performance function*, namely, the mapping from the set of act-names to {1,0}, then we may put down the following semantical rules:

III. Semantical rules

i) An act α is either performed or not performed, that is $f(\alpha) = 1$ or $f(\alpha) = 0$.

ii) $f(\ulcorner \sim \alpha \urcorner) = 1$ if $f(\alpha) = 0$; otherwise $f(\ulcorner \sim \alpha \urcorner) = 0$.

iii) $f(\ulcorner [\alpha \& \beta] \urcorner) = 1$ if $f(\alpha) = 1$ and $f(\beta) = 1$; otherwise, $f(\ulcorner [\alpha \& \beta] \urcorner) = 0$.

iv) $f(\ulcorner [\alpha \vee \beta] \urcorner) = 1$ if either $f(\alpha) = 1$ or $f(\beta) = 1$; otherwise, $f(\ulcorner [\alpha \vee \beta] \urcorner) = 0$.

v) $f(\ulcorner [\alpha \supset \beta] \urcorner) = 1$ if either $f(\alpha) = 0$ or $f(\beta) = 1$; otherwise, $f(\ulcorner [\alpha \supset \beta] \urcorner) = 0$.

vi) $f(\ulcorner [\alpha \equiv \beta] \urcorner) = 1$ if either $f(\alpha) = 1$ and $f(\beta) = 1$ or $f(\alpha) = 0$ and $f(\beta) = 0$; otherwise, $f(\ulcorner [\alpha \equiv \beta] \urcorner) = 0$.

6. When expressions are listed in separate lines, no single quotes will be used. For example, (2.1) should otherwise be written as: (2.1) 'If an act is obligatory, ...'.

The list may be regarded as a set of semantical rules for the deontic connectives. To avoid the difficulty in talking about acts, let us associate the performance value (which is originally associated with acts) from now on with act names.[7] It is easy to see that the performance value of a molecular act name is uniquely determined by the performance values of its constituent atomic act names. We may call the former a *performance function* of the latter. This is a departure from von Wright's formulation, for he says that "An *act* will be called a performance-function of certain other acts, if its performance-value...uniquely depends upon the performance-values of those other acts..."[8]

Here we have an analogue of truth function in propositional logic. Von Wright even pushes this analogy a little further by calling $\ulcorner \sim\alpha \urcorner$, $\ulcorner [\alpha \& \beta] \urcorner$, $\ulcorner [\alpha \vee \beta] \urcorner$, $\ulcorner [\alpha \supset \beta] \urcorner$ and $\ulcorner [\alpha \equiv \beta] \urcorner$, a *negation-act,* a *conjunction-act,* a *disjunction-act,* an *implication-act,* and an *equivalence-act,* respectively. We shall, however, prefer to call the last two a *conditional-act* and a *biconditional-act,* respectively.

Let Ω be a *deontic evaluation function* from the set of act names to the set $\{1^*, 0^*\}$ where '1*' denotes permission, and '0*' denotes non-permission, i.e., forbiddance. These two are called the *deontic values.* If the deontic value of a molecular act name is uniquely determined by the deontic values of its component act names, then the

---

7 This is hardly a new practice. We find philosophers, notably Leonard, apply the predicate 'true' both to a *sentence* (Leonard calls it a statement) and a *proposition.* Thus, a sentence may be defined as true if and only if the proposition it indicates is true. Cf. Leonard [1967], §§ 5.3f.

8 Von Wright [1951a], p. 2. My italics.

former is said to be a *deontic function* of the latter. It should be noted that not every molecular act name is a deontic function of its component names.[9] In other words, deontic function does not in general coincide with performance function. For instance, from the fact that α is permissible, it is not determined whether $\ulcorner \sim\alpha \urcorner$ is permissible or not permissible. It may be the case that both an act and its negation-act are permissible, or it may be the case that only one of them is. However, just as a disjunction-act name has the performance value performance ("1") if and only if at least one of its component act names has the performance value performance, a disjunction-act has the deontic value permission ("1*") if and only if at least one of its component act names has the deontic value permission. We are thus able to establish the following:

IV. $\Omega (\ulcorner [\alpha \vee \beta] \urcorner) = 1^*$ if $\Omega (\alpha) = 1^*$ or $\Omega (\beta) = 1^*$; otherwise,
 $\Omega (\ulcorner [\alpha \vee \beta] \urcorner) = 0^*$

This means that in the case of a disjunction-act name, deontic function and performance function coincide. This provides us with a way of establishing a decision procedure for deontic (logical) truth in system vW.

In order to outline this decision procedure, let us first put down von Wright's two basic principles in this system. One of them can be inferred from what we have just said above. Another principle is justifiable offhand by our intui-

---

9 Again, von Wright defines a deontic function as a relation on acts rather than on act names. We find him saying: "An act will be called a deontic function of certain other acts, if the deontic value of the former uniquely depends upon the deontic values of the latter" and "...not any act which is a performance-function of certain acts is also a deontic function of them." *Ibid.*, p. 6.

tive notion of permission.

(2.4) *Principle of permission*: "Any given act is either itself permitted (permissible) or its negation is permitted (permissible)". [10] Hence, for every a, either 'Pa' is true or 'P$\sim a$' is true.

(2.5) *Principle of deontic distribution for permission*: If α is '$(a_1 \, \text{v} a_2 \, \text{v}...\text{v}a_n)$', [11] then $\ulcorner P\alpha \urcorner$ is true if and only if '$(Pa_1 \, \text{v}Pa_2 \, \text{v}...\text{v}Pa_n)$' is true. Von Wright's version: "If an act is the disjunction of two other acts, then the proposition that the disjunction is permitted is the disjunction of the proposition that the first act is permitted and the proposition that the second act is permitted (This principle can, naturally, be extended to disjunctions with any number n of members)". [12]

Let us now proceed to explain our decision procedure. Let A be any arbitrary P-sentence, atomic or molecular, in system vW; let A_1, A_2,...,A_k be a complete list of atomic (P-) sentences appearing in A. Clearly A is a truth function of A_1, A_2, ...,A_k. Now, each A_i in the list $A_1, A_2,...A_k$ is of the form $\ulcorner P\alpha_i \urcorner$, [13] where α_i may be an atomic or a molecular name. Let us assume further that 'a_1', 'a_2',..., 'a_n' is a complete list of atomic names occurring in A, that is, in either A_1 or A_2 or ...or A_k. As a first step toward the decision procedure, we shall construct a complete disjunctive normal

10 *Ibid.*, p. 9.

11 We shall follow the usual convention on the omission of grouping indicators, and we shall use parentheses as substitutes for brackets, thinking of the former as poorly-drawn versions of the latter.

12 *Ibid.*, p. 7. Von Wright's own parenthetical remarks.

13 The use of the same subscript 'i' in both $\ulcorner A_i \urcorner$ and $\ulcorner P\alpha_i \urcorner$ is harmless. We do this for the sake [of facilitating the subsequent presentation.

form δ^i of each α_i relative to the complete list of atomic names 'a$_1$', 'a$_2$',..., 'a$_n$' appearing in A, except when α_i is contradictory. In that case we write α_i as 'a & $\sim a$'. This special case will be treated later. Meanwhile let us suppose that no α_i is contradictory. Thus, each δ^i is a disjunction $\ulcorner\delta_1^i \text{ v } \delta_2^i v...v\delta_r^i\urcorner$ ($1 \leq r \leq 2^n$) in which each δ_j^i is a conjunction $\ulcorner\beta_1 \& \beta_2 \& ... \& \beta_n\urcorner$ where each β_m ($1 \leq m \leq n$) is either 'a$_m$' or '$\sim$a$_m$'. Now, just as in propositional logic a formula has the same truth value as its complete disjunctive normal form, in system vW a name has the same performance value as its complete disjunctive normal form. This comes from the fact that performance function, as we saw above, resembles truth function in a straightforward way. Consequently, each A$_i$, that is Pα_i can be written as

(2.6) $P(\delta_1^i v \delta_2^i v...v\delta_r^i)$

But the truth value of (2.6) is, according to (2.5) above, the same as

(2.7) $P\delta_1^i v P\delta_2^i v...v P\delta_r^i$

Let us call each $P\delta_j^i$ ($1 \leq j \leq r$) in (2.7) a *P-constituent* of (2.6), and hence of Pα_i, that is, A$_i$. And we shall call (2.7) a *P-disjunction* of A$_i$.

When each A$_i$ (i=1,2,...,k) of A has been written as a P-disjunction, we may establish a complete list of (distinct) P-constituents $\ulcorner P\phi_1\urcorner$, $\ulcorner P\phi_2\urcorner$,..., $\ulcorner P\phi_s\urcorner$ ($1 \leq s \leq 2^n$) of A as the set consisting of those and only those P-constituents which appear in the P-disjunction of any of the A$_i$ of A. Now, since A is a truth function of A$_1$, A$_2$,...,A$_k$, and each A$_i$ of A is, among other things, a truth function of its P-constituents. It follows that A is a truth function of its complete list of P-constituents.

A decision procedure is now immediately visible. Let

A be an arbitrary P-sentence we want to examine, let $\ulcorner P\phi_1 \urcorner$, $\ulcorner P\phi_2 \urcorner$,..., $\ulcorner P\phi_s \urcorner$ be a complete list of P-constituents of A. We shall construct a truth table for A in the usual fashion except that on the upper part (row) of the (left-side) assignment columns we list the complete list of P-constituents $\ulcorner P\phi_1 \urcorner$, $\ulcorner P\phi_2 \urcorner$,..., $\ulcorner P\phi_s \urcorner$ of A instead of the complete list of variables as we commonly do in propositional logic. On the upper row of (right-side) evaluation columns, we put down A* which is exactly like A except each A_i thereof is replaced by its P-disjunction $P\delta_1^i v\, P\delta_2^i v...vP\delta_r^i$. It is easy to see that A* is truth functionally equivalent to A. We then proceed to put down all the possible combina-tion of truth values, i.e., 't' 's and 'f' 's, under the list $\ulcorner P\phi_1 \urcorner$, $\ulcorner P\phi_2 \urcorner$,..., $\ulcorner P\phi_s \urcorner$ in the assignment columns, with a restric-tion we shall mention later. After the assignment columns are thus furnished with 't' 's and 'f' 's, we shall evaluate each row of the truth table in the familiar way by appeal-ing to the semantical rules of propositional logic until finally we come up with the truth values for the main connective of A*. If we have all 't' 's under it, then A*, and hence A, expresses a deontic (logical) truth. We shall call it a *deontic tautology* of system vW, or a *vW-tautology*. Otherwise, A is not a vW-tautology.

Now, the special case we mention earlier. If any α_i is contradictory, and thus we write it as '$a \,\&\sim a$', then the decision procedure goes essentially the same as above said except that we now have some occurrence (s) of '$P(a\&\sim a)$' in A* which is to be evaluated. In a truth table we simply put an 'f' under '$P(a\&\sim a)$' in every row in the evaluation column, and go ahead to further evaluation. The rationale of doing this is that a P-sentence is true if and only if at least one of its P-constituents is true. But now 'P$(a \& \sim a)$' has no P-constituent, hence it is always false.

Of course, what we have outlined above is only a decision procedure applicable to a P-sentence. However, since other deontic sentences, i.e., O-sentences, F-sentences, and I-sentences, are all definable in terms of P-sentences, we have *mutatis mutandis* a decision procedure applicable to any deontic sentence.

Let us give an example to show what a truth table looks like. Suppose we want to examine the following sentence,

(2.8) $Fa \supset O(a \supset b)$

we first rewrite it as a P-sentence of vW, that is

(2.9) $\sim Pa \supset \sim P \sim (a \supset b)$

Let us call it A which consists of two atomic (P-) sentences, namely, 'Pa' and 'P$\sim (a \supset b)$'. The name 'a' appearing in the first atomic sentence can be put into its complete disjunctive normal form relative to the complete list of atomic names occurring in A, namely, 'a' and 'b', as '$(a \& b)$ v $(a \& \sim b)$; and the name '$\sim (a \supset b)$' appearins in the second atomic sentence can be similarly rendered as '$\sim \sim (a \& \sim b)$' which is the same as '$(a \& \sim b)$'. Now, rewrite 'Pa' and 'P$\sim (a \supset b)$' as their P-disjunctions. We have '[P$(a \& b)$ v P$(a \& \sim b)$]' and 'P$(a \& \sim b)$', respectively. Thus, A* of A is the following sentence

(2.10) $\sim [P(a \& b)$ v $P(a \& \sim b)] \supset \sim P(a \& \sim b).$

The following truth table constructed in the above-described manner shows that (2.10) is a vW-tautology. (In this case, we have 'P$(a \& b)$' and 'P$(a \& \sim b)$' as a complete list of P-constituents of A).

P $(a\,\&\,b)$	P $(a\,\&\sim b)$	$\sim$ (P $(a\&b)$ v P $(a\&\sim b)$)				⊃	$\sim$ P $(a\&\sim b)$	
t	t	f	t	t	t	t	f	t
f	t	f	f	t	t	t	f	t
t	f	f	t	t	f	t	t	f
f	f	t	f	f	f	t	t	f

Since we have 't' 's and only 't' 's under the main connective '⊃' of A*, A* is a vW-tautology. Consequently,
A is a vW-tautology. That is to say, (2.8) abbreviates a
sentence which is a vW-tautology.

However, in using this truth-tabular method, one restriction must be observed. This restriction can be laid
down as follows. Suppose, 'a_1', 'a_2', ..., 'a_n' is a complete
list of distinct atomic names appearing in A, then we *might*
have less than or equal to 2^n distinct P-constituents $\ulcorner P\phi_1\urcorner$,
$\ulcorner P\phi_2\urcorner$, ..., $\ulcorner P\phi_s\urcorner$ of A. If the number of P-constituents
of A is 2^n, i.e., $s = 2^n$ then, in the assignment column, the
row in which all $\ulcorner P\phi_i\urcorner$'s are assigned falsehood should be
deleted from the truth table. For example, if A is 'Pa v
P$\sim a$ v Pb v P$\sim b$', then we have *two* distinct atomic
names, 'a' and 'b'. After the above-mentioned manipulation,
A can be shown as being equivalent to

(2.11)   P $(a\,\&\,b)$ v P $(a\,\&\sim b)$ v P $(\sim a\,\&\,b)$ v
            P $(\sim a\,\&\sim b)$

Here we have $2^2 = 4$ distinct P-constituents, hence the foregoing restriction applies. The truth table for (2.11) then
looks like

$P(a\&b)$	$P(a\&\sim b)$	$P(\sim a\&b)$	$P(\sim a\&\sim b)$	......
t	t	t	t	
f	t	t	t	
t	f	t	t	
f	f	t	t	
t	t	f	t	
f	t	f	t	
t	f	f	t	
f	f	f	t	
t	t	t	f	
f	t	t	f	
t	f	t	f	
f	f	t	f	
t	t	f	f	
f	t	f	f	
t	f	f	f	

There is no additional row in which we have straight 'f' 's across the evaluation columns.

The rationale behind this restriction is easily seen from the principle of permission, i.e., (2.4) together with the principle of deontic distribution for permission, i.e., (2.5). When all the 2^n P-constituents are false, we have

(2.12) $\sim P\,(a_1 \& a_2 \& a_3 \&...\& a_n) \ \&\sim P\ (\sim a_1 \& a_2$
          $\& a_3 \&......\& a_n) \ \&...\&\sim P\ (a_1 \& a_2 \&...$
          $\& a_{n-1} \&\sim a_n)$

That is

(2.13) $\sim [P\,(a_1 \& a_2 \& a_3\&...\& a_n) \lor P\,(\sim a_1 \& a_2 \& a_3$

$$\&...\& \; a_n) \; v...v \; P (a_1 \& a_2 \&...\& a_{n-1} \&\sim a_n)]$$

This by (2.5) is equivalent to

(2.14) $\sim [P (a_1 \& a_2 \& a_3 \&...\& a_n) \; v \; (\sim a_1 \& a_2 \& a_3 \&...$
                $...\& a_n) \; v \; (a_1 \&\sim a_2 \& a_3 \&...\& a_n) \; v...$
                $v \; (a_1 \& a_2 \&...\& a_{n-1} \&\sim a_n)]$

But (2.14) by propositional logic (henceforth: PL) is the same as

(2.15) $\sim [P (a_1 \; v \sim a_1) \& (a_2 \; v \sim a_2) \&...\& (a_n \; v \sim a_n)]$

which, by (2.5) again, is

(2.16) $\sim [(Pa_1 \; v \; P \sim a_1) \& (Pa_2 \; v \; P \sim a_2) \&...$
                $...\& (Pa_n \; v \; P \sim a_n)]$

That is,

(2.17) $\sim (Pa_1 \; v \; P \sim a_1) \; v \sim (Pa_2 \; v \; P \sim a_2) \; v...$
                $...v \sim (Pa_n \; v \; P \sim a_n)$

This contradicts (2.4) which reads: for every a_i, either Pa_i or $P \sim a_i$.

This restriction can also be intuitively justified as fol-lows. Suppose the restriction is violated, then from what we have just demonstrated, it follows that an act and its negation-act are both forbidden (not permissible). This, by definitions (D 1.1) and (D 1.2) above, means in turn that both an act and its negation-act are obligatory. An assertion at direct variance with our intuition.

The following are some of the deontic tautologies in system vW. We use '$\vdash A$' to mean that A is a deontic tautology.

(Th. 1) $\vdash Pa \equiv \sim O \sim a$ (a is permissible if and only if not-a is not obligatory.)

(Th. 2) $\vdash Pa \equiv \sim Fa$ (a is permissible if and only if a is not forbidden.)

(Th. 3) $\vdash Oa \supset Pa$ (If a is obligatory, then a is permissible)

(Th. 4)   ⊢F∼a⊃Pa (If not-a is forbidden, then a is permissible) .

(Th. 5)   ⊢O(av∼a) (a-or-not-a is obligatory) .

(Th. 6)   ⊢F(a &∼a) (a-and-not-a is forbidden) .

(Th. 7)   ⊢∼(Oa & O∼a) (It is not the case that a is obligatory and not-a is also obligatory) .   ˙

(Th. 8)   ⊢O(a & b) ≡.Oa & Ob (a-and-b is obligatory if and only if a is obligatory and b is obligatory) .

(Th. 9)   ⊢Oa v Ob. ⊃O(a v b) (If either a is obligatory or b is obligatory, then a-or-b is obligatory.

It may be remarked in passing that 'v' here is to be understood as strictly analogous to the 'v' in propositional logic. From 'p v q' we are not entitled to infer 'p'. Likewise, from 'O(a v b)' we cannot jump to the conclusion 'Oa' Otherwise, (Th. 9) above and (Th. 10) below become very curious deontic laws. [14]

(Th. 10)   ⊢O(a &∼a) ⊃Ob (If a-and-not-a is obligatory, then any b is obligatory) .

(Th. 11)   ⊢P(a v b) ≡. Pa v Pb (a-or-b is permissible if and only if either a is permissible or b is permissible) .

(Th. 12)   ⊢Oa & O(a⊃b). ⊃Ob (If a is obligatory and a-only-if-b is obligatory, then b is obligatory) .

(Th. 13)   ⊢Pa & O(a⊃b). ⊃Pb (If a is permissible and a-only-if-b is obligatory, then b is permissible.)

(Th. 14)   ⊢Fb & O(a⊃b). ⊃Fa (If b is forbidden and

---

14 For the meaning of 'v' or 'or' in deontic logic or imperative logic, see § 31.

a-only-if-b is obligatory, then a is forbidden.)

(Th. 15) $\vdash (Fb \ \& \ Fc) \ \& \ O[a \supset (bvc)].\supset Fa$ (Similarly)

(Th. 16) $\vdash \sim[O(a \ v \ b) \ \& \ (Fa\&Fb)]$ (Similar to (Th. 7))

(Th. 17) $\vdash Oa \ \& \ O[(a \ \& \ b) \supset c].\supset O(b \supset c)$ (similar to (Th. 12))

(Th. 18) $\vdash Fa \supset O(a \supset b)$ (If a is forbidden, then a-only-if-b is obligatory).

(Th. 19) $\vdash Ob \supset O(a \supset b)$ (If b is obligatory, then a-only-if-b is obligatory).

§3. THE PARADOXES OF "DERIVED OBLIGATION"

In [1951a] and [1951b], von Wright proposed to formulate in system vW another moral concept which seems important and far-reaching in a moral discussion, namely the concept of moral commitment or derived obligation. According to him, the concept of doing something that *commits* us to do something else could be analyzed into the concept of obligation and that of a conditional-act. He made the analysis in the following way:

(3.1) Doing one act a commits us to do another act b if and only if the conditional-act $a \supset b$ is obligatory.

Thus moral commitment is defined in terms of obligation and conditional-acts. For example, if making a promise commits us to keep it then the conditional-act if-promise-making-then-promise-keeping is obligatory. This analysis, at first sight, seems natural and sound enough. For it says that it is obligatory that either a promise is not made or else it is kept, thus answering very closely to our intuitive notion of a moral commitment. However, if we read this notion of commitment uniformly into the theorems of system vW, then some strange and even counter-intuitive results appear.

Consider the following two theorems:

(Th. 18) $\vdash Fa \supset O(a \supset b)$

(Th. 19) $\vdash Ob \supset O(a \supset b)$

(Th. 18) says, without going into the concept of commitment, that if the act a is forbidden, then it is obligatory that either a is not done or b is done. And (Th. 19) says, likewise, that if b is obligatory, then it is obligatory either not to do a or to do b. Both theorems, under this interpretation, appear to be harmless and indeed plausible and are thus welcomed by our intuition. But once we read '$O(a \supset b)$' as "doing a commits us to do b" into them, then these two theorems become, respectively,

(3.2)   If a is forbidden, then doing it commits us to do any act b.

and

(3.3)   If b is obligatory, then doing any act a commits us to do b.

That is to say, doing a forbidden act commits us to do any arbitrary act, and any arbitrary act commits us to do an obligatory act. These statements, especially the first one, seem counter-intuitive or "paradoxical". For, according to (Th. 18), breaking a promise (presumably a forbidden act) commits us, among other things, to murder (of course, also commits us not to murder). This certainly worries us very much. (Th. 18) and (Th. 19) have thus been called the "paradoxes" of derived obligation or the paradoxes of commitment.[1]

G. H. Hughes suggests that we formalize "doing a commits us to do b" not as "$O(a \supset b)$'" but as '$a \supset Ob$'.[2] Of course, this formula, as it stands, is not well-formed

---

[1] These two theorems, which resemble the so-called paradoxes of strict implication in alethic modal logic, were first pointed out by Prior [1954].

[2] See Prior [1962]. p. 224.

in von Wright's original version of vW. However, we can reformulate the formation rules of it to accommodate Hughes' formula. Under this new formulation, the first paradox disappears, for 'Fa ⊃ (a ⊃ Ob)' is no longer a theorem in this widened system vW$^+$.[3] But the second one abides, because 'Ob ⊃ (a ⊃ Ob)' is simply a theorem of propositional logic.

Von Wright himself made a more dramatic proposal. He thought that just as modal logic is inadequate to formalize the concept of entailment, the formalization of the

---

[3] We may construct a mixed truth table to show that 'Fa ⊃ (a ⊃ Ob)', that is, '~Pa ⊃ (a ⊃ ~P~b)', or '~[P(a & b) v P(a & ~b)] ⊃ {a ⊃ ~[P (a & ~b) v P(~a & ~b)]}', is not a deontic tautology in system vW$^+$:

P(a&b)	P(a&~b)	P(~a&~b)	a	~[P(a&b) v P(a&~b)] ⊃ {a⊃~[P(a&~b) v P(~a&~b)]}
t	t	t	t	• • • • • • • • • • •
f	t	t	t	• • • • • • • • • • •
t	f	t	t	• • • • • • • • • • •
f	f	t	t	t f f f f t f f f t t
t	t	f	t	• • • • • • • • • • •
f	t	f	t	• • • • • • • • • • •
t	f	f	t	• • • • • • • • • • •
f	f	f	t	• • • • • • • • • • •
t	t	t	f	• • • • • • • • • • •
f	t	t	f	• • • • • • • • • • •
t	f	t	f	• • • • • • • • • • •
f	f	t	f	• • • • • • • • • • •
t	t	f	f	• • • • • • • • • • •
f	t	f	f	• • • • • • • • • • •
t	f	f	f	• • • • • • • • • • •
f	f	f	f	• • • • • • • • • • •

concept of moral commitment cannot be accomplished within system vW. [4] He thus proposed a new system of deontic logic in which the concept of permission is relativized in the following way. We now speak not of some act's being permissible or not, but rather, of its being permissible or not under certain condition. We let 'P(a, c)' mean that act a is permissible under condition c. This is a relative notion of permission, or as it is sometimes called, *conditional permission*. And 'P' is used here as a binary deontic predicate rather than a singulary one as we saw in system vW.

Other deontic concepts, i.e., obligation, forbiddance and indifference can be similarly relativized. The relation among them can be depicted by definitions strictly analogous to (D 2.1) — (D 2.3) in last section, namely

(D 3.1) $\quad \ulcorner O(\alpha, \delta) \urcorner =_{Df} \ulcorner \sim P(\sim \alpha, \delta) \urcorner$

(D 3.2) $\quad \ulcorner F(\alpha, \delta) \urcorner =_{Df} \ulcorner \sim P(\alpha, \delta) \urcorner$

(D 3.3) $\quad \ulcorner I(\alpha, \delta) \urcorner =_{Df} \ulcorner (P(\alpha, \delta) \ \& \ P(\sim \alpha, \delta)) \urcorner$

This deontic system of conditional permission of von Wright will be called 'CvW'. [5]

The following are two additional axioms of CvW given by von Wright himself: [6]

(A 3.1) $\quad$ P(a, c) v P$(\sim a, c)$

(A 3.2) $\quad$ P$(a \& b, c) \equiv$ P(a, c) & P(b, c)

Von Wright made the following proposal for the formulation of the concept of commitment. He said that a

---

4 See von Wright [1951b], p. 9, and [1956], p. 509.

5 There are other deontic systems based on conditional permission. For example, the system developed in Rescher [1958].

6 Von Wright [1956], p. 509. He had not given a complete list of axioms for system CvW.

necessary condition for saying that doing an act commits us to do another act is that the latter is obligatory under the condition that the former is done. [7] That is to say, if doing a commits us to do b, then $O(a, b)$ is the case. Now, since the following two formulas, as he claimed, are not theorems of CvW [8]

(3.4) $F(a, cv{\sim}c) \supset O(b, a)$

(3.5) $O(a, cv{\sim}c) \supset O(a, b)$

the paradoxes are thus avoided in the system CvW of conditional permission. Of course, the question still remains whether we are able to avoid these paradoxes without going into the relativization of deontic concepts or whether similar paradoxes arise within CvW.

It may be noted in passing that the notion of "absolute permission", that is, the notion of permission formalized in system vW, can be reformulated in terms of the conditional permission of system CvW. For we may write '$P(a, cv{\sim}c)$' to stand for 'Pa' where $cv{\sim}c$ may be called a tautologous condition, that is, a condition which is ever-present. In other words, to say that something is absolutely permissible is to say that it is permissible under any condition whatsoever.

---

7 Von Wright, *ibid*.

8 We are not in a position to prove von Wright's claim, because the complete primitive basis of system CvW was not given.

§4. CONTRARY-TO-DUTY IMPERATIVES AND CHISHOLM'S DILEMMA

Deontic logic, as we pointed out earlier, is meant to capture certain deontic concepts and formalize them in a systematic way. The success of a certain deontic logician may thus be judged, at least partially, by how well his system will accommodate these concepts. For example, it is reasonable for us to demand that a deontic logician must try to develop a deontic system which will accommodate as thoroughly and as successfully as possible all the concepts which we intuitively conceive as deontic. If a system of deontic logic fails to incorporate a certain deontic concept satisfactorily, we may think it defective in that respect. One example is the case of commitment we have mentioned earlier in conncection with system vW in which von Wright's original proposal of formulating the notion of commitment leads to paradoxical, and hence unsatisfactory, results. The following is another example.

Roderick M. Chisholm [1963a] first pointed out that deontic logics formulated in the manner of system vW suffer another drawback. This fly in the ointment, which can also be found in systems OT*—OS5* and Anderson's OM—OM", [1] can be described as follows. In system vW and other similar systems we cannot formulate the concept which Chisholm called the *contrary-to-duty* imperative adequately

---

[1] See §§ 6-12.

without getting into undesirable results.

To see the problem, let us proceed as follows. First of all, it is easily observed that human beings are not morally perfect. A man violates from time to time certain moral codes, or neglects consciously or unconsciously certain ethical duties. Hence, our moral rules may often be couched in such a way that will both allow and dictate a reparative course of action. For instance, one of our moral rules, when rendered explicit, may have the following schema:

(4.1)   One ought to do so and so; but if one, for some reason or other, fails to do it, one ought, by all means, to do such and such. [2]

This schema may even be generalized to read:

(4.2)   One ought to do so and so; but if one, for some reason or other, fails to do it; one ought, by all means, to do such and such; but if one again, for some reason or other, fails to do it, one ought, by all means, to do...; but if one again, for some reason or other, fails to do it, one ought, by all means, to do thus and thus.

However, for some practical reasons which are easily conceived, this chain of restorative clauses will not extend very long. It must soon stop somewhere. But exactly at what point our moral rules cease to prescribe any further reparative course of action seems largely to depend upon what kind of morality is involved and what situation we are in. But we are not going to discuss these issues any further

---

2 Chisholm, in [1963a], p. 33. put forward the following formulation: "You ought to do *a*, but if you do not do *a*, then you must, by all means, do *b*."

as they will certainly lead us too far away from our principal concern of this section.

The desirability, if not indispensability, of including reparative clauses in our moral rules is easily understandable if not immediately obvious. For one thing, human beings are far from being morally incorruptible, as we mentioned above. One may, at sometime or other, do something wrong in full awareness. If our moral rules admit no restitution of any kind, they leave no room for a man to make a compensation for his wrong-doing. This type of unreparable morality may sometimes even drive a man who has done something wrong into a corner and make him lead an evil life henceforth. Another reason for welcoming the type of morality that has room for reparation is this. Most of our moral rules, unlike the *jus scriptum,* are not explicitly put down. Quite often, if not as a rule, we have to work on a trial-and-error basis in order to see whether or not our course of action complies with the vaguely conceived moral rules. In short, to act morally requires not only the will to be moral but also the intelligence and insight. And it is needless to say that to err is human. Therefore, it seems rather unreasonable to advocate an absolute morality which allows no violations and offers no chance of restitution of any kind.

These are, then, some of the reasons for the admittance of the reparative course of action in our moral life expressed by contrary-to-duty imperatives. [3] Hence, it is no wonder

---

3 There are other reasons for reparative morality. For instance, a man may not be in a position adequate for the fulfillment of his duty. This relates itself to the question whether "ought" always implies "can" in every sense of this word. We shall come across this question later.

that we want to see a deontic system accommodate this concept well and to our expectation. But, as we mentioned earlier, Chisholm has shown that system vW and other similar systems fail in this respect. To see this, let us use Chisholm's example. [4]

Let us suppose that, according to our moral rules, it is obligatory for a man to go to the assistance of his neighbors, and it is also obligatory that if he goes he tells them he is coming. Now, suppose further that the moral rules also prescribe that if he does not go, then he is forbidden to tell them that he is coming (i. e., that it is obligatory that he does not tell them that he is coming), and, furthermore, let it be the case that the man, at variance with his duty, does not go. In order to see how this situation introduces a difficulty into a deontic system such as vW or vW$^+$, let us express the foregoing assumptions in terms of the language of vW$^+$. Let 'a' denote the act of going to his neighbor's assistance, 'b' denote that of telling them he is coming. Then we have the following:

(4.3) Oa (a is obligatory)

(4.4) $O(a \supset b)$ (It is obligatory that if-a-then-b)

(4.5) $\sim a \supset O \sim b$ (If not-a, then it is obligatory not-b)

and

(4.6) $\sim a$ (Not-a, or a is not done)

It is known that formulas like (4.5) are not well-formed in system vW. Hence, what it purports to describe cannot be expressed in system vW. That is to say, system vW cannot handle this particular kind of state of affairs which (4.5) describes from the very beginning. However, it has

---

4 *Ibid.*, pp. 34-35.

also been indicated that this system can be reformulated into system vW^+ which will admit formulas such as (4.5) as well-formed. Let us assume that we are talking about system vW^+.

In system vW^+, it can be easily shown that
(4.7) $Oa \& O(a \supset b) . \supset Ob$
That is, (Th. 12) of system vW, remains a theorem.[5] And since *modus ponens* is supposed to be desirable rule of inference in ordinary deontic systems, we can infer from (4.3), (4.4) and (4.7) the following
(4.8) Ob (b is obligatory)
But from (4.5) and (4.6) we have
(4.9) $O \sim b$ (Not-b is obligatory)
Hence we have, by rule of adjunction, the following:
(4.10) $Ob \& O \sim b$ (b is obligatory and not-b is obligatory)
However, the following formula is provable in vW^+, indeed it is a theorem, i.e., (Th. 7), of vW;
(4.11) $\sim (Ob \& O \sim b)$ (It is not the case that b is obligatory and not-b is obligatory)
We have a patent contradiction. We have, therefore, the following dilemma. Either the system, as in the case of vW, cannot formulate the concept of contrary-to-duty imperative, or else, it contains a contradiction. We shall call it *Chisholm's dilemma*.

---

5 Von Wright's truth-tabular method suffices to show that it is a theorem.

§ 5. DEONTIC LOGIC AND MODAL LOGIC

In von Wright's original treatment ([1951a] and [1951b]), deontic concepts such as "obligatoin", "permission", "forbiddance," and "indifference" are said to be modal concepts quite on a par with alethic concepts like "necessity". "possibility"; epistemic concepts "verification", "falsification", "undecidedness" and existential concepts "universality", "existence" and "emptiness". Indeed he has pointed out from time to time the similarity and dissimilarity among these four different groups of modal concepts. For instance, comparing deontic concepts with alethic concepts we find the following striking resemblance. We observe, on the one hand, that what is necessary is possible and what is impossible is necessarily not the case; we have, on the other hand, what is obligatory is permissible, and what is not permissible is obligatory not to do. However, this happy similarity cannot be pushed very far. For instance, although it is commonly held that what is necessary is the case, we hardly need to point out the falsity that what is obligatory is done. It is because of this not very pervasive resemblance that we find von Wright saying that "there are essential similarities but also characteristic differences between the various groups of modalities. They all deserve, therefore, a special treatment." [1]

1 Von Wright [1951a], p. 1.

Indeed he treated alethic modalities, epistemic modalities and deontic modalities separately and each to a fairly great extent in [1951a] and [1951b]. Later when he made further contributions to deontic logic, he conceived it as a quite independent discipline without making further efforts to bring other branches of "modal logics" into consideration. However, he did look into the possibility that deontic logic might find its basis on another theory, e.g., on a certain type of tense logic. [2]

But other logicians and philosophers are evidently deeply impressed by the above-mentioned similarity between deontic concepts and alethic concepts. They think it deserves far more than our passing attention. They reason that if we reinterpret certain operators and variables in alethic modal logic in such a way that a well-formed formula in this system becomes a well-formed formula of deontic logic, and then take away from the alethic modal logic certain theorems which do not hold in deontic logic, then what we obtain is a system of deontic logic based upon alethic modal logic. So far much effort has been made in this direction, and we have now in the literature quite a few systems of deontic logic built up in this way. Among the logicians who have made contributions in this respect we find the well-known names: Anderson, Castañeda, Fisher, Fitch, Kripke, Lemmon, and Prior.

In what follows, we shall try to make a preliminary remark on how to construct a system of deontic logic in the above-mentioned fashion. In the next few sections

---

2 See, for example, von Wright [1965b] and [1966]; also Åqvist [1966]. Compare with Halldēn [1951] and Åqvist [1963c]. Cf. § 14.

three systems of deontic logic OT*, OS4* and OS5* based, respectively, on modal logics T, S4 and S5 will be examined. Comparison will be made between these systems and von Wright's vW or, rather, a special version vW* of vW, Fisher-Åqvist's system FÅ and Anderson's systems OM— OM″. While we are making a survey of these systems we shall remind ourselves of those deontic problems we have so far mentioned and indicate some further problems.

First of all, let us suppose that we have a system of standard propositional logic, say Church's system P_2.[3] We will call it "PL". A (propositional) modal logic may then be built up by adding to PL certain vocabulary, formation rules, axioms and/or rules of inference. For instance, the following primitive basis depicts a modal logic which is commonly called system T.[4]

I. Vocabulary
  i) An infinite supply of propositional variables: 'p', 'q', 'r', 'p_1', 'q_1', 'r_1', 'p_2',...
  ii) Two singulary sentential connective: '∼', '□'.
  iii) A binary sentential connective: '⊃'.
  iv) Two grouping indicators: '[', ']'.

II. Formation rules
  i) A propositional variable standing alone is a wff (well-formed formula).
  ii) If A and B are wffs, so are ⌜∼A,⌝ ⌜[A⊃B]⌝ and ⌜□A.⌝
  iii) Nothing else is a wff.

3 See Church [1956], p. 119ff, or Massey [1969], part II.
4 See Feys [1937—1938]. This system is deductively equivalent to, or has the same theorems as, von Wright's system M in [1951b]. This result is proved by Sobociński [1953].

III. Rules of inference
    (R1) Substitution
    (R2) *modus ponens.*
    (R3) Necessitation.

Other sentential connectives includindg the modal ones are defined in the usual way. For instance,

    (D5.1) $\ulcorner \Diamond A \urcorner =_{Df} \ulcorner \sim \Box \sim A \urcorner$

Again, we will follow the common practice in the omission of grouping indicators, and later the use of parentheses as poorly drawn brackets.

IV. Axioms
    (A1) $\vdash p \supset [q \supset p]$
    (A2) $\vdash [p \supset [q \supset r]] \supset [[p \supset q] \supset [p \supset r]]$
    (A3) $\vdash [\sim q \supset \sim p] \supset [p \supset q]$
    (A4) $\vdash \Box [p \supset q] \supset [\Box p \supset \Box q]$
    (A5) $\vdash \Box p \supset p^5$

    It is well known that by adding
    (A8) $\vdash \Box p \supset \Box \Box p$

to the above primitive basis for system T, we obtain a system called S4. And if we add instead the following axiom

    (A9) $\vdash \sim \Box p \supset \Box \sim \Box p$

then, the result is a system known as S5.

    Let us denote the primitive basis of system T as { (R1) - (R3), (A1) - (A5) } leaving its vocabulary and formation rules understood. By the same token, { (R1) - (R3), (A1) - (A5), (A8) } is the primitive basis of S4, and so on.

---

5 (A1) - (A3) for propositional logic is due to Łukasiewicz. See Łukasiewicz and Tarski [1930], p. 35 (note 9). This is a simplification of Frege's six axioms in *Begriffsschrift*, 1879.

Due to the similarity between our intuitive concept of necessity and that of obligation on the one hand, and between our concept of possibility and that of permission on the other, it is quite natural that people try to reinterpret the two alethic modalities '$\Box p$' and '$\Diamond p$' as "p is obligatory" and "p is permissible", respectively. Indeed, this deontic reinterpretation of alethic modalities seems so interesting and far-reaching that it has thus far received much attention from logicians. A small example may help indicate our preliminary confidence in this reinterpretation. Suppose that we take (D5.1) and reinterpret accordingly the two modalities it contains. Then we get a deontic counterpart

(D5.2) $\ulcorner PA \urcorner = {}_{Df} \ulcorner \sim O \sim A \urcorner$

which is certainly welcomed by our intuition.

Strictly speaking, however, (D5.2) cannot be said to express the same idea of defining one deontic modality in terms of another as what is expressed by, say (D2.1) - (D2.3) of § 2. The deontic modalities which (D5.2) and (D2.1) talk about are really two different kinds. In (D2.1), a deontic modality under consideration is an expression consisting of a deontic predicate followed by a name for act, while in (D5.2), a deontic modality, on the other hand, is an expression composed of a deontic operator but followed rather by a name for a proposition. In general, if we try to reinterpret the primitive basis of a modal logic, say system T, in the manner stated above, we are constructing a deontic system of a different type from the one we discussed in § 2, namely Von Wright's system vW. In vW, as we recall, a deontic predicate applies to an act name. But now in a deontically reinterpreted modal system, instead of act names we have proposition names which are proper operands of the deontic operators. Thus what are now said to be obligatory, permissible and the like are no longer acts but propositions. This deviation from von Wright's original conception of deontic modality need not give us too much trouble. For we can readily understand a deontic formula like

(5.1)   Op

as meaning

(5.2)   The realization of p is obligatory.

or, perhaps more conventionally

(5.3)   To bring it about that p is obligatory.

where 'p' denotes a proposition, or if we like, a state of affairs.

This type of deontic logic is much favored in the recent development. Von Wright has himself adopted this general line of practice, too, although he does it in a slightly more specific form. [6] This renewed conception of deontic modality is not immune to every difficulty. But, for the time being, we shall simply assume its workability until later in the next chapter.

When we reinterpret the modal system T, S4 and S5 deontically in the manner explained above, it involves the change of '□' to 'O' throughout the axioms and rules of inference in the foregoing systems. Consequently, we have:

(A1) - (A3)   (same)

(Ad4) $\vdash O\,(p \supset q) \supset (Op \supset Oq)$

(Ad5) $\vdash Op \supset p$

(Ad8) $\vdash Op \supset OOp$

---

[6] He lets the individual variables denote so-called "generic states of affairs". See, for example, [1963b], [1964] and [1967b].

(Ad9) $\vdash \sim Op \supset O \sim Op$

(R1) - (R2)   (same)

(Rd3)   Deontic necessitation: from A we may infer $\ulcorner OA \urcorner$.

Now, corresponding to modal system T, S4 and S5, we may define three deontic systems OT, OS4 and OS5 which have, respectively, the following primitive basis: { (A1) - (A3), (Ad4) - (Ad5), (R1) - (R2), (Rd3) }, { (A1) - (A3), (Ad4) - (Ad5), (Ad8), (R1) - (R2), (Rd3) }, and { (A1) - (A3), (Ad4) - (Ad5), (Ad9), (R1) - (R2), (Rd3) }.

However, these deontic systems are intolerably counter-intuitive (from our point of view, of course) because of the presence of (Ad5) which, when rendered into our everyday language, reads

(5.4)   If something ought to be done, then it is done. This certainly does not describe the moral phenomena we daily experience, because in our world it seems quite obvious that the following is true:

(5.5)   There is something which ought to be done but, as a matter of fact, is not done.

Note that (5.4) and (5.5), when carefully reformulated, are directly in contradiction to each other. Hence, any deontic system which includes (Ad5) and thus asserts (5.4) must be rejected as totally unnatural and inadequate to our world. Indeed, any system of deontic logic containing (Ad5) may be objected from another point of view. Suppose that (Ad5) can be asserted, then by (R1) we have

(5.6) $O \sim p \supset \sim p$

This, by a usual definition, i.e., (D5.2), becomes

(5.8) $p \supset Pp$

That is,

(5.9)　　　If something is done, then it is permissible.

(5.4) and (5.8) then entail that no duties are neglected and nothing forbidden is done. A world with this property may be called a *morally perfect world* because in such a world there is no sin but there is every virtue provided that to sin is forbidden and to be virtuous is obligatory. [7] But in a world like this, people will not have much interest in deontic logic because of its triviality. For instance, OT, OS4 and OS5 are nothing but special interpretations (or models) of T, S4 and S5, respectively. Therefore, deontic concepts reveal no special characteristics of themselves. They are only copy images of alethic modal concepts. In this case, deontic laws coincide with alethic modal laws.

It may be noted in passing that although we call a world in which (5.4) and (5.9) hold a morally perfect world, this should not lead us to think that in such a world it is also true that

(5.10)　　　A non-obligatory thing is not done.

To assert (5.10) is to assert

(5.11)　　　$\sim Op \supset \sim p$

or, equivalently,

(Ad10)　　　$p \supset Op$

And since we know that (Ad10) cannot be proved in OT, OS4 or OS5, [8] we have to add it as an axiom. But by adding this axiom to these systems, the following becomes provable.

---

[7] It may be the case that, under some moral rules, not every virtue is obligatory. Cf. Chisholm [1963b].

[8] This can be shown by any of the decision procedures known for T, S4 and S5.

(5.12) $Op \equiv p$

A world having this property may be called a *strictly virtuous world* in that not only is every virtue present but also every non-virtue is absent provided that, according to the morality of this world, it is obligatory to live virtuously. Note also that the morality of such a world may be thought of as logically trivial. Because when (5.12) is provable in a deontic system, then that system simply collapses into the usual propositional logic. Thus, the deontic laws strictly coincide with the propositional logical laws. This, again, makes the construction of deontic logic superfluous.

Since (Ad5) is unwelcome in deontic logic as we have just shown, let us delete it from the primitive bases of OT, OS4 and OS5. Instead we add to each of these systems the following two weaker axioms: [9]

(Ad6) $\vdash Op \supset \sim O \sim p$

(Ad7) $\vdash O[Op \supset p]$

The resulting systems will be called OT*, OS4* and OS5*', respectively. And we define a system OS5* as the system which results from adding (Ad8), i.e., '$Op \supset OOp$', to OS5*'. [10]

Axiom (Ad6) is a highly desirable one, because it is,

---

[9] Similar axiom-set can be found, for example, in Hanson [1965].

[10] The reason for defining OS5* in this manner rather than calling OS5*' OS5* is to preserve the nice property that OS5* contains OS4* just as OS4* contains OT*. Another way of obtaining OS5* would be the addition of the following axiom to OS5*'

(Ad11) $\vdash O[p \supset Op]$

However, to do this would mean to explicitly postulate a morally excessive rigorism, so to speak, in that what is done ought to be that which ought to be done. This leaves no room for morally in-different acts.

by (D5.2), equivalent to

(5.13) $Op \supset Pp$

That is,

(5.14)   If something is obligatory, then it is permissible. As to (Ad7), there may be someone who will frown on it mainly because of the iteration of deontic modality. It is not clear, for example, what we mean when we say that it is obligatory that it is obligatory to do such and such.[11] However, there are logicians, notably Prior, who contend that (Ad7) is harmless, or indeed welcome, in deontic logic. [12] For it reads intuitively

(5.15)   It ought to be the case that what ought to be done be done.

which seems not only innocent but also desirable.

Another reason against the acceptance of (Ad7) is expressed by Feys. [13] He observes that in some systems of modal logic, particularly Lewis' modal systems S1-S5, (A5), i.e. '$\Box p \supset p$' can be proved from the alethic counterpart of (Ad7), namely, from

(Ad7) $\vdash \Box [\Box p \supset p]$

But the deontic counterpart of (A5), that is (Ad5), is to be rejected. Hence, Feys suggests that we delete, among other things, (A7) or its deductive equivalent from Lewis' systems and replace it with certain other axioms in order to obtain intuitively satisfactory deontic logics.

---

11 It may be recalled that deontic formulas containing interated deontic modalities are not well-formed in system vW.

12 See, for example, Prior [1956], p. 86f.

13 In "Expression modale du «devoir-être»." An abstract from the Amsterdam Meeting of the Associaton for Symbolic Logic. *Journal of Symbolic Logic*, vol. 20, 1955, pp. 91-92.

It is true that from (A7) we can prove (A5) in any of Lewis' systems provided that we use the following two rules:

> (R6) Strict detachment: From A and $\ulcorner \Box[A \supset B]\urcorner$ to infer B.
>
> (R7) Replacement of strict equivalents.

As Prior notes the proof can be carried out in any of Lewis' systems. [14] Since system T is known to contain S2, [15] the proof can also be obtained in system T.

However, some logicians, Prior is one of them, contend that it is unsatisfactory to exclude (Ad7) from deontic logic. [16] They lay the blame of the deducibility of (A5) from (A7) on (R6) and (R7) rather than on (A7). In-deed, it is easily seen that the deontic counterparts of these two rules—call them (Rd6) and (Rd7), respectively—are not sound rules in deontic logic. For from so and so is the case and it is obligatory that if so and so is the case then such and such is the case, we cannot correctly infer that such and such is the case. Likewise, from it ought to be the case that so and so is the case if and only if such and such is the case, there is no warranty that 'so and so' and 'such and such' are then interchangeable in any deontic formula. Prior offhand rejects these two rules. As to the latter rule, i.e., (Rd7), he makes the following remarks:

"There seems to be the same intuitive objectionableness about the rule permitting substitution of strict equivalents,

---

14 For the proof, see Prior, *ibid.*, p. 87.

15 See, for example, Feys [1965], p. 124.

16 Prior, *ibid.*, p. 87. Also, Anderson: "Review of A. N. Prior's A Note on the Logic of Obligation and Feys' Reply", *Journal of Symbolic Logic*, vol. 21, 1956, p. 379.

when this is interpreted deontically, that is, when it is taken to mean that if α *ought to* imply and be implied by β, then α and β *are* interchangeable in any formula. This is optimism, too, is it not? I cannot think immediately of a counter-example to it...." [17]

The following simple example may be of the same kind that he has in mind. Suppose, according to a set of moral rules, that it is the case that

(5.16)   It ought to be the case that if one violates a moral rule, then one is punished.

(5.17)   It ought to be the case that one is punished only if one violates a moral rule.

and

(5.18)   It is permissible that one be punished.

From (5.16) - (5.18) one may not be able to infer that

(5.19)   It is permissible that one violates a moral rule.

17 Prior, *ibid.*, p. 87. His italics.

§ 6. DEONTIC LOGICS AS "SUBSYSTEMS" OF MODAL LOGIC

For the sake of clarity, let us, first of all, summarize the primitive bases of three deontic systems we just arrived at, namely, OT*, OS4* and OS5*. Again, we shall omit the vocabulary and formation rules.

The following rules of inference are laid down for all three systems:

(R1)   Substitution.

(R2)   *modus ponens.*

(R3)   Deontic necessitation.

For system OT* we put down the following axioms:

(A1) $\vdash p \supset [q \supset p]$

(A2) $\vdash [p \supset [q \supset r]] \supset [[p \supset q] \supset [p \supset r]]$

(A3) $\vdash [\sim q \supset \sim p] \supset [p \supset q]$

(Ad4) $\vdash O[p \supset q] \supset [Op \supset Oq]$

(Ad6) $\vdash Op \supset \sim O \sim p$

(Ad7) $\vdash O[Op \supset p]$

If we add:

(Ad8) $\vdash Op \supset OOp$

we have system OS4*. And if we add to system OS4* the following

(Ad9) $\vdash \sim Op \supset O \sim Op$

the result is system OS5*.

Other sentential connectives are defined as usual. And the following definitions are common to all three systems:

(Dd1) $\ulcorner PA \urcorner =_{Df} \ulcorner \sim O \sim A \urcorner$

(Dd2) $\ulcorner FA \urcorner =_{Df} \ulcorner \sim PA \urcorner$

(Dd3) $\ulcorner IA \urcorner =_{Df} \ulcorner PA \& P \sim A \urcorner$

Here $\ulcorner IA \urcorner$ may be rendered as "A is (morally) indifferent".

It may be pointed out that by adding (Ad5), that is, 'Op⊃p', to OT*, OS4* and OS5* we obtain OT, OS4 and OS5, respectively. This can be seen by showing that (Ad6) and (Ad7) are derivable in OT, OS4, and OS5. [1] This means that OT*, OS4* and OS5* are, respectively, sub-systems of OT, OS4 and OS5. But OT, OS4 and OS5, as constructed in the last section, are exactly the same as T, S4 and S5, respectively, except where there is an 'O' in the former we have a'□' in the latter. We shall say that the former are, respectively, the deontic variants of the latter, and the latter, the alethic variants of the former.

The following chart shows the containing relation among some of the systems we have just mentioned:

---

1 The proof of (Ad7) is trivial, since we have (Ad5) and (Rd3). It is also straightforward to show that (Ad6) is provable in those systems. We may sketch the proof as follows:

(1)   ⊢Op⊃p   (Ad5)

(2)   ⊢[q⊃∼r]⊃[r⊃∼q]   PL

(3)   ⊢[O∼p⊃∼p]⊃[p⊃∼O∼p]   Substitution   (Henceforth: Sub.) (2)

(4)   ⊢O∼p⊃∼p   Sub. (1)

(5)   ⊢p⊃∼O∼p   (3) (4) *modus ponens* (hereafter: MP)

(6)   ⊢[p⊃q]⊃[[q⊃r]⊃[p⊃r]]   PL

(7)   ⊢[Op⊃p]⊃[[p⊃∼O∼p]⊃[Op⊃∼O∼p]]   Sub. (6)

(8)   ⊢Op⊃∼O∼p   (1) (5) (7) Two uses of MP

Note: in our proofs we shall make free use of simultaneous substitution and replacement of equivalents in propositional logic. They are, as well-known, derived rules on the basis {(A1) – (A3), (R1) – (R2)}.

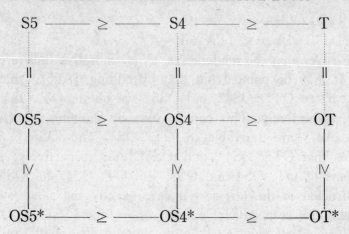

where 'S_1——$\geq$——S_2' means that system S_1 contains system S_2, and 'S_1——$=$——S_2' means S_1 contains and is contained by S_2, i.e., S_1 and S_2 are mutually containing or equivalent. On the other hand, we let 'S_1 ⋯⋯ $\geq$ ⋯⋯ S_2' and 'S_1 ⋯⋯ $=$ ⋯⋯ S_2' mean, respectively, the same as 'S_1——$\geq$ ——S_2' and 'S_1——$=$——S_2' except that in the former S_1 and S_2 may contain different designs of symbols. For example, one is the deontic variant (which contains 'O') of the other which is an alethic system (that contains '□' instead).

We shall next exhibit some of the theorems in our deontic systems. First of all, the theorems of system OT*. Needless to say, all theorems of OT* are also theorems of OS4*, and all theorems of OS4* are also theorems of OS5*.

The following are theorems which show the "material equivalence" between certain O-sentences, P-sentences, F-sentences and I-sentences:

(OT*1) $\vdash OP \equiv \sim P \sim p$ (p is obligatory if and only if not-p is not permissible)

Pf. (1) ⊢p≡~~p PL

(2) ⊢Op≡~~OP Sub. (1)

(3) ⊢O~~p≡~~O~~p Sub. (2)

(4) ⊢Op≡~P~p   (3),(Dd1), PL

(OT*2) ⊢Op≡ F~p (p is obligatory if and only if not-p is forbidden)

Pf. (1) ⊢Op≡~P~p   (OT*1)

(2) ⊢Op≡F~p   (1),(Dd2)

(OT*3) ⊢Pp≡~Fp (p is permissible if and only if p is not forbidden)

Pf. (1) ⊢Pp≡~~Pp PL

(2) ⊢Pp≡~Fp   (1),(Dd2)

(OT*4) ⊢Pp≡~O~p (p is permissible if and only if not-p is not obligatory)

Pf. Similarly, (Dd1)

(OT*5) ⊢Fp≡~Pp (p is forbidden if and only if p is not permissible)

Pf. (OT*3), PL

(OT*6) ⊢Fp≡O~p (p is forbidden if and only if not-p is obligatory)

Pf. (OT*4), (Dd2), PL

(OT*7) ⊢O~p≡~Pp (Not-p is obligatory if and only if p is not permissible)

Pf. (OT*5), (OT*6), PL

(OT*8) ⊢P~p≡~Op (Not-p is permissible if and only if p is not obligatory)

Pf. (OT*1), PL

(OT*9) ⊢F~p≡~P~p (Not-p is forbidden if and only if not-p is not permissible)

Pf. (OT*5), PL

From the above nine theorems, we may list the following twelve mutual transformations between different deontic sentences. We denote each of them by (T1), (T2), ..., (T12) so that we can refer to them later in our proofs of other theorems. These transformations are:

(T1)   ⌜OA⌝ «⋯⋯» ⌜~P~A⌝

(T2)   ⌜~OA⌝ «⋯⋯» ⌜P~A⌝

(T3)   ⌜O~A⌝ «⋯⋯» ⌜~PA⌝

(T4)   ⌜~O~A⌝ «⋯⋯» ⌜PA⌝

(T5)   ⌜PA⌝ «⋯⋯» ⌜~FA⌝

(T6)   ⌜~PA⌝ «⋯⋯» ⌜FA⌝

(T7)   ⌜P~A⌝ «⋯⋯» ⌜~F~A⌝

(T8)   ⌜~P~A⌝ «⋯⋯» ⌜F~A⌝

(T9)   ⌜FA⌝ «⋯⋯» ⌜O~A⌝

(T10)   ⌜~FA⌝ «⋯⋯» ⌜~O~A⌝

(T11)   ⌜F~A⌝ «⋯⋯» ⌜OA⌝

(T12)   ⌜~F~A⌝ «⋯⋯» ⌜~OA⌝

(OT*10) ⊢Ip≡. Pp & P~p (p is indifferent if and only if p is permissible and not-p is also permissible)

  Pf. (1) ⊢Pp & P~p.≡.Pp & P~p   PL

       (2) ⊢Ip≡. Pp & P~p   (1),(Dd3)

The following theorems are those that show the "material implication" between deontic sentences:

(OT*11) ⊢Op⊃Pp (If p is obligatory, then p is permissible)

  Pf. (Ad6),(Dd1)

There follow from (OT*11) togehter with (T1)—(T12) the following five additional theorems:

(OT*12) ⊢O~p⊃~Op (If not-p is obligatory, then p is not obligatory)

(OT*13) $\vdash \sim Pp \supset P \sim p$ (If p is not permissible, then not-p is permissible)

(OT*14) $\vdash Fp \supset \sim Op$ (If p is forbidden, then p is not obligatory)

(OT*15) $\vdash Fp \supset \sim F \sim p$ (If p is forbidden, then not-p is not forbidden)

(OT*16) $\vdash F \sim p \supset Pp$ (If not-p is forbidden, then p is permissible)

It is easily seen that the above sixteen theorems are common to every system of deontic logic in which (Dd1) — (Dd3) are incorporated and in which classical propositional logic is presupposed.

(OT*17) $\vdash O (p \lor \sim p)$ (p-or-not-p is obligatory)

Pf. (1) $\vdash p \lor \sim p$ PL

(2) $\vdash O (p \lor \sim p)$ (1), (Rd3)

In general, we can prove

(6.4) $\vdash Ot$

where 't' stand for a tautology. That is to say, to realize a tautology is obligatory.

(OT*18) $\vdash F (p \& \sim p)$ (p-and-not-p is forbidden)

Pf. (1) $\vdash O (p \lor \sim p)$ (OT*17)

(2) $\vdash O \sim (p \& \sim p)$ (1), PL

(3) $\vdash F (p \& \sim p)$ (2), (T9)

Likewise, we have, in general, the following as a theorem:

(6.5) $\vdash Ff$

where 'f' stands for a contradiction. That is to say, to actualize a contradiction is forbidden.

Some philosophers may frown at (6.4) and (6.5) and hence at (OT*17) and (OT*18), because these theorems imply that our moral code makes a prescription, among other things, concerning the act that people logically cannot help doing, i.e., the "tautologous act" and the act that people logically cannot do, i.e., the "contradictory act". It seems more natural to have our moral code say nothing on these "logical acts", because they are not intentional acts, and someone may claim that only intentional acts are subject to moral judgment.

The same point may be viewed, perhaps more convincingly, from another angle. That is, to consider the corresponding examples in imperative logic. Suppose a person is requested to do a contradictory act, he will never be able to fulfill it no matter how hard he tries; and if he is ordered to carry out a tautologous act, he needs to do nothing and the order is automatically executed. Now, we may ask: Is the request a genuine request, and the order a real one?

We shall leave this question aside without making any attempt to answer it. Meanwhile, we might think of the unnaturalness of (OT*17) and (OT*18) as one of the expenses we pay for our deontic systems.

(OT*19) below is not new to us. It seems indeed a truism in deontic logic.

$$(OT^*19) \quad \vdash \sim (Op \,\&\, O\sim p) \quad \text{(It is not the case that p is}$$
obligatory and not-p is also obligatory)

Pf. (1) $\vdash Op \supset \sim O\sim p$ (Ad6)

(2) $\vdash \sim Op \,v\sim O\sim p$ (1), PL

(3) $\vdash \sim (Op \,\&\, O\sim p)$ (2), PL

However, this theorem reminds us of Chisholm's dilemma which we dealt with earlier. That is, this dilemma again threatens us in systems OT*, OS4* and OS5* just as it does in system vW or vW⁺.

From (OT*19) and (T1) — (T12) the following two

theorems come as immediate consequences:

(OT*20)   ⊢Pp v P∼p (Either p is permissible or not-
           p is permissible)

(OT*21)   ⊢∼ (Op & Fp) (It is not the case that p is
           both obligatory and forbidden)

Let us prove, at this point, a derived rule to the following effect:

(Rd4)   If ⊢⌜A⊃B⌝, then ⊢⌜OA⊃OB⌝
        Pf.   (1) ⊢A⊃B   Assumption
              (2) ⊢O(A⊃B)   (1), (Rd3)
              (3) ⊢O(p⊃q) ⊃. Op⊃Oq   (Ad4)
              (4) ⊢O(A⊃B) ⊃. OA⊃OB   Sub. (3)
              (5) ⊢OA⊃OB   (2) (4), MP

As we shall witness soon, this rule facilitates from
time to time the proofs of many subsequent theorems.

The following are theorems in which molecular names
are involved.

(OT*22)   ⊢O(p &∼p) ⊃Oq (If p-and-not-p is obliga-
           tory, then any q is obligatory)
           Pf.   (1) ⊢p &∼p.⊃q   PL
                 (2) ⊢O(p &∼p) ⊃Oq   (1),(Rd4)

(OT*23)   ⊢Op⊃O(p v q) (If p is obligatory, then p-
           or-q is obligatory)
           Pf.   Similar to that of (OT*22) [Hereafter:
                 Similar: (OT*22)]

(OT*24)   ⊢Pp⊃P(p v q) (If p is permissible, then p-
           or-q is permissible)
           Pf.   (1) ⊢∼ (p v q) ⊃∼p   PL
                 (2) ⊢O∼ (p v q) ⊃O∼p   (1),(Rd4)
                 (3) ⊢∼O∼p⊃∼O∼ (p v q)   (2), PL
                 (4) ⊢Pp⊃P(p v q)   (3),(Dd1)

(OT*25) $\vdash Fp \supset F(p\,\&\,q)$ (If p is forbidden, then p-and-q is forbidden)

Pf.   Similar: (OT*24)

(OT*26) $\vdash F(p \lor q) \supset Fp$ (If p-or-q is forbidden, then p is forbidden)

Pf.   (OT*24), PL, (T6)

(OT*27) $\vdash O(p\,\&\,q) \equiv.\ Op\,\&\,Oq$ (p-and-q is obligatory if and only if p is obligatory and q is obligatory)

Pf.   (1) $\vdash p\,\&\,q.\supset p$ PL

(2) $\vdash O(p\,\&\,q) \supset Op$ (1),(Rd4)

(3) $\vdash O(p\,\&\,q) \supset Oq$ Similarly

(4) $\vdash O(p\,\&\,q) \supset.\ Op\,\&\,Oq$ (2) (3),PL

(5) $\vdash p \supset (q \supset.\ p\,\&\,q)$ PL

(6) $\vdash Op \supset O(q \supset.\ p\,\&\,q)$ (5),(Rd4)

(7) $\vdash O(p \supset q) \supset.\ Op \supset Oq$ (Ad4)

(8) $\vdash O(q \supset.\ p\,\&\,q) \supset.\ Oq \supset O(p\,\&\,q)$ Sub. (7)

(9) $\vdash Op \supset (Oq \supset O(p\,\&\,q))$ (6) (8),PL

(10) $\vdash Op\,\&\,Oq. \supset O(p\,\&\,q)$ (9),PL

(11) $\vdash O(p\,\&\,q) \equiv.\ Op\,\&\,Oq$ (4) (10), PL

(OT*28) $\vdash P(p \lor q) \equiv.\ Pp \lor Pq$ (p-or-q is permissible if and only if p is permissible or q is permissible)

Pf.   (OT*27), PL, (T3)

(OT*29) $\vdash F(p \lor q) \equiv.\ Fp\,\&\,Fq$ (p-or-q is forbidden if and only if p is forbidden and q is forbidden)

Pf.   (OT*28), PL, (T6)

(OT*30) $\vdash O(p \lor q) \supset.\ Pp \lor Pq$ (If p-or-q is obligatory, then either p is permissible or q is permissible)

Pf. (1) ⊢Op⊃Pp   (OT*11)

    (2) ⊢O (p v q) ⊃ P (p v q)   Sub. (1)

    (3) ⊢P (p v q) ≡. Pp v Pq   (OT*28)

    (4) ⊢O (p v q) ⊃. Pp v Pq   (2) (3), PL

(OT*31) ⊢P (p & q) ⊃. Pp & Pq (p-and-q is permissible only if p is permissible and q is permissible)

    Pf. (1) ⊢Pp⊃P (p v q)   (OT*24)

    (2) ⊢P (p & q) ⊃P ((p & q) v (p &∼q))

    Sub. (1)

    (3) ⊢P (p & q) ⊃Pp   (2), PL

    (4) ⊢P (p & q) ⊃Pq   Similarly

    (5) ⊢P (p & q) ⊃. Pp & Pq   (3) (4), PL

(OT*32) ⊢Op v Oq. ⊃O (p v q)   (If either p is obligatory or q is obligatory, then p-or-q is obligatory)

    Pf. (OT*23), PL

(OT*33) ⊢Fp⊃O (p⊃q)   (If p is forbidden, then if-p-then-q is obligatory)

    Pf. PL, (Rd4), (T9)

(OT*34) ⊢Oq⊃O (p⊃q)   (If q is obligatory, then if-p-then-q is obligatory)

    Pf. PL, (Rd4)

These two theorems, according to the reading quoted above, are quite innocuous. (OT*33) says that if to bring it about that p is forbidden, then either-not-to-bring-it-about-that-p-or-to-bring-it-about-that-q is obligatory. Or, roughly speaking, if doing one thing is forbidden, then it is obligatory either not to do it or to do something else. And this seems quite acceptable to our intuition. Likewise, (OT*34) may be similarly rendered. And the result is again unobjectionable. However, if we use ⌜O (A⊃B)⌝ to express commitment as we saw in § 3. then the paradoxical results are immediately seen. Actually, (OT*33) and (OT*34) are exactly the same, respectively, as (Th. 18) and (Th. 19) of system vW except the difference in individual variables. And the latter theorems have been called the paradoxes of derived obligation. That means that our systems do not escape the defects we found in system vW in association with these paradoxes.

(OT*35) $\vdash Op \,\&\, O\,(p \supset q)\,.\, \supset Oq$ (If p is obligatory and if-p-then-q is obligatory, then q is oblig-atory)

      Pf.   (1) $\vdash (p \,\&.\, p \supset q) \supset q$ PL

             (2) $\vdash O\,(p \,\&\, (p \supset q)) \supset Oq$ (1), (Rd4)

             (3) $\vdash O\,(p \,\&\, q) \equiv.\, Op \,\&\, Oq$ (OT*27)

             (4) $\vdash O\,(p \,\&\, (p \supset q)) \equiv.\, Op \,\&\, O\,(p \supset q)$
                   Sub. (3)

             (5) $\vdash Op \,\&\, O\,(p \supset q)\,.\, \supset Oq$ (2) (4), PL

(OT*36) $\vdash Pp \,\&\, O\,(p \supset q)\,.\, \supset Pq$ (If p is permissible and if-p-then-q is obligatory, then q is per-missible)

      Pf.   PL, (Rd4), (OT*30), (T3)

(OT*37) $\vdash Fq \,\&\, O\,(p \supset q)\,.\, \supset Fp$ (If q is forbidden and if-p-then-q is obligatory, then p is forbidden)

      Pf.   (OT*36), PL, (T6)

(OT*38) $\vdash (Fq \,\&\, Fr) \,\&\, O\,(p \supset (q \lor r))\,.\, \supset Fp$ (If q is forbidden and r is forbidden and if-p-then-(q-or-r) is obligatory, then p is forbidden)

      Pf.   (OT*37), PL, (OT*29)

(OT*39) $\vdash \sim (O\,(p \lor q) \,\&\, (Fp \,\&\, Fq))$ (It is not the case that p-or-q is obligatory, yet p is forbidden and q is forbidden)

Pf.   (1) ⊢ ~ (Op & Fp)   (OT*21)
    (2) ⊢ ~ (O (p v q) & F (p v q))   Sub. (1)
    (3) ⊢ F (p v q) ≡. Fp & Fq   (OT*29)
    (4) ⊢ ~ (O (p v q) & (Fp & Fq))   (2) (3),
       PL

(OT*40)   ⊢OP & O ((p & q) ⊃ r) . ⊃ O (q ⊃ r)   (Similar
    to (OT*38))
    Pf.   (OT*35), PL

It may be observed that many of the theorems listed here are variant theorems of system vW. They differ only in style of variables. Indeed, this coincidence is not accidental. We shall, in the next section, prove that every theorem of system vW is a variant theorem of system OT*. Of course, the converse is not true.

Before closing this section, let us prove another derived rule of our system (s).

(Rd5)   If ⊢⌜A ⊃B⌝, then ⊢⌜PA ⊃ PB⌝
The proof is straightforward:
    Pf.   (1) ⊢A ⊃ B   Assumption
       (2) ⊢ ~B ⊃ ~A   (1),PL
       (3) ⊢O~B ⊃ O~A   (2),(Rd4)
       (4) ⊢ ~O~A ⊃ ~O~B   (3),PL
       (5) ⊢PA ⊃ PB   (4),(T4)

Again, this rule will be used on certain occasions to facilitate our proofs.

§7. SYSTEMS OT*, vW AND FÅ

To show that system vW of section 2 is a variant subsystem of OT*, we shall first axiomatize a variant system vW* of vW as follows.

I. Vocabulary

Same as vW except that we now have as individual variables 'p' 'q', 'r', 'p₁', 'q₁', 'r₁' 'p₂',... which range over propositions and that we now include not only 'P' but also 'O', 'F', and 'I' as deontic predicates.

II. Formation rules

Similar to that of vW. Here we have not only P-sentences, but also O-sentences, F-sentences, and I-sentences.

III. Axioms

(A1) $\vdash p \supset [q \supset p]$
(A2) $\vdash [p \supset [q \supset r]] \supset [[p \supset q] \supset [p \supset r]]$
(A3) $\vdash [\sim q \supset \sim p] \supset [p \supset q]$
(Ad6) $\vdash Op \supset \sim O \sim p$
(OT*28) $\vdash P(p \vee q) \equiv . Pp \vee Pq$

IV. Rules of inference

(R1)   Substitution.
(R2)   *modus ponens*.
(Rd6)   P-extensionality: From $\ulcorner A \equiv B \urcorner$ we may infer $\ulcorner PA \equiv PB \urcorner$.

This axiomatization is essentially Prior's restatement of

principles listed by von Wright in [1951a] and [1951b],[1] except that we have here a different type of individual variables and that some parts of this systematization are not explicitly mentioned in Prior's formulation.

It is readily seen that all the axioms of vW* are either axioms or theorems of OT*. Besides, the first two rules of inference are exactly the same as the first two rules of OT*. The only thing that remains to be seen is that (Rd6), which is the only thing new in this system, can be derived in OT*. But this is obvious, because the rule is entailed by, and indeed is a weaker version of, (Rd5) of OT*. It follows that every theorem of vW* is also a theorem of OT*.

To show that the converse does not hold, we need only to present an example which is a theorem of OT* but not a theorem of vW*. As we know, trivially (Ad7), i.e., 'O(Op⊃p)' is a theorem of OT*. Nevertheless, it is not a theorem, indeed not even a well-formed formula, of vW*. This concludes the proof that system vW* is a (proper) subsystem of OT*.

Now, system vW* and system vW are otherwise the same except in two respects. First, these two systems have different individual variables as we have seen above. Secondly, in vW* we have 'O', 'P', 'F' and 'I' as deontic predicates, while in vW we have only 'P'. (This is also true for system OT*). It follows that what is a theorem of vW* might only be an abbreviation of a theorem of vW. For example, 'Op⊃Pp' is a theorem of vW*, but only '∼P∼p⊃Pp' is a variant theorem of vW

---

1 See Prior [1962], p. 221.

(or OT*). If we keep this latter difference in mind, and are willing to tolerate the discrepancy as we did above, we might as well say that system vW, like system vW*, is a variant (proper) subsystem of system OT*. But since this discrepancy is sometimes unnegligibly important as we shall see in section 12 we might want to say that vW, like vW*, is a variant quasi-subsystem of OT*, meaning that what is a theorem of the former may only be an abbreviation of a theorem of the latter, or *vice versa* (what is an abbreviation of a theorem of the former is a theorem of the latter).

It has been mentioned that (OT*1) — (OT*16) are theorems common to every deontic logic of the common type, namely, one in which we have (Dd1) — (Dd3), (A1) — (A3) and (R1) — (R2). And now we have shown that vW* is a proper subsystem of OT*. But these remarks are not to be taken as in the least suggesting that OT* is a system comprehensive enough to accommodate every deontic theorem one might expect, even if we agree to let the deontic logic be developed along the lines set out by von Wright in system vW.

In what follows we shall reconstruct and examine a deontic system FÅ which was first proposed by M. Fisher and later amended by L. Åqvist. [2] This system, like vW, takes the set of acts as the range of the individual variables. But, unlike the latter, it possesses the following new feature found neither in vW nor in OT*, i. e., FÅ is a three-valued system. This system, similar to vW but unlike OT*, has a finite characteristic matrix.

First, the primitive basis of system FÅ.

---

2 Fisher [1961b] and Åqvist [1963b].

I. Vocabulary

  i) Deontic variables: 'a', 'b', 'c', 'a₁',...
  ii) Deontic connectives: 'N', 'K', 'A', 'C', 'E'
  iii) Sentential connectives: '~', '&', 'v', '⊃' '≡'
  iv) Deontic predicates: 'P', 'O', 'F', 'I'

II. Formation rules

  i) Every deontic variable is a deontic name.
  ii) If α and β are deontic names, so are $\ulcorner N\alpha \urcorner$, $\ulcorner K\alpha\beta \urcorner$, $\ulcorner A\alpha\beta \urcorner$, $\ulcorner C\alpha\beta \urcorner$ and $\ulcorner E\alpha\beta \urcorner$.
  iii) Nothing else is a deontic name.
  iv) If α is a deontic name, then $\ulcorner P\alpha \urcorner$, $\ulcorner O\alpha \urcorner$, $\ulcorner F\alpha \urcorner$ and $\ulcorner I\alpha \urcorner$ are wffs (atomic).
  v) If A and B are wffs, so are $\ulcorner \sim A \urcorner$, $\ulcorner [A \& B] \urcorner$, $\ulcorner [A v B] \urcorner$, $\ulcorner [A \supset B] \urcorner$, and $\ulcorner [A \equiv B] \urcorner$ (molecular).
  vi) Nothing else is a wff.

The axiomatization of this system is available. [3] However, since the value-table type of decision procedure is handy, [4] we shall follow this approach.

III. Semantics

Instead of putting down a set of rather lengthy semantical rules, we shall present, as Fisher and Åqvist did, a set of matrices to capture the semantics of this system. We let '0', '1' and '2' stand for the deontic values "obligatoriness", "indifference" and "forbiddance", respectively. The set of matrices can then be given as follows:

A) For deontic names

---

3 This has been worked out by Åqvist, *ibid*. See Appendix I.
4 First presented by Fisher, *ibid*. and revised by Åqvist, *ibid*.

α	N
0	2
1	1
2	0

K	β 0	1	2
$\alpha\{$ 0	0	1	2
1	1	1	2
2	2	2	2

A	β 0	1	2
$\alpha\{$ 0	0	0	0
1	0	1	1
2	0	1	2

C	β 0	1	2
$\alpha\{$ 0	0	1	2
1	0	1	1
2	0	0	0

E	β 0	1	2
$\alpha\{$ 0	0	1	2
1	1	1	1
2	2	1	0

B) For atomic wffs

α	Oα	Pα	Fα	Iα
0	t	t	f	f
1	f	t	f	t
2	f	f	t	f

C) For molecular wffs

The usual fundamental truth tables for '$\sim$', '&', 'v', '$\supset$', and '$\equiv$'.

A deontic tautology of FÅ, or an FÅ-tautology, may be defined in the usual way, namely, that a wff is a tautology if it is true under every value assignment. Since the consistence and completeness of FÅ have been proved by Åqvist, we have the following result:

(7.1)   A is a theorem of FÅ if and only if A is an

FÅ-tautology.

To serve as an illustration, we shall use the above matrices to show that (Th. 18) of system vW is also a theorem of FÅ. In order to shorten the calculation, we follow Fisher in the employment of Quine's truth value analysis. [5]

(Th. 18) $\vdash Fa \supset OCab$ (If a is forbidden, then if-a-then-b is obligatory)

Pf. $a=1$ $F1 \supset OC1b$

$\qquad\qquad f \underset{\tau}{\supset} OC1b$

Similarly when a=0, 2

Hence, (Th. 18) is an FÅ-tautology. By (7.1) it is a theorem of FÅ.

Likewise, we can show that (Th. 19) and (Th. 7) of vW are again theorems of FÅ. It follows that system FÅ, just as OT* and vW, is plagued by the nightmare of the paradoxes of derived obligation and Chisholm's dilemma, if we want to formulate commitment in terms of obligation and the conditional.

Systems FÅ and OT* share many theorems. Or, more strictly speaking, many theorems of this system are variant theorems of that system. For instance, the variants of the following theorems of OT* are all FÅ-tautologies, and hence theorems of FÅ.

(OT*41) $\vdash Fp \& Fq. \supset F(p \& q)$ (If p is forbidden and q is forbidden, the p-and-q is forbidden)

Pf.   (1) $\vdash \sim p \supset \sim (p \& q)$ PL

$\qquad$ (2) $\vdash O \sim p \supset O \sim (p \& q)$ (1), (Rd4)

---

[5] Quine [1950], § 5, pp. 22ff.

$\quad$ (3) $\vdash p \supset q . \supset . \ p \supset (r \supset q)$ $\quad$ PL

$\quad$ (4) $\vdash O \sim p \supset O \sim (p \& q) . \supset . O \sim P \supset$
$\qquad (O \sim q \supset O \sim (p \& q))$ $\quad$ Sub. (3)

$\quad$ (5) $\vdash O \sim p \supset (O \sim q \supset O \sim (p \& q))$ $\quad$ (2)
$\qquad$ (4), PL

$\quad$ (6) $\vdash (O \sim p \& O \sim q) \supset O \sim (p \& q)$ $\quad$ (5),
$\qquad$ PL

$\quad$ (7) $\vdash Fp \& Fq . \supset F(p \& q)$ $\quad$ (6), (T9)

(OT*42) $\vdash Fp \& Oq . \supset F(p \& q)$ (If p is forbidden and q is obligatory, then p-and-q is forbidden) Pf. (OT*25), PL

(OT*43) $\vdash Fp \& Iq . \supset F(p \& q)$ (If p is forbidden and q is indifferent, then p-and-q is forbidden) Pf. Similar: (OT*43)

(OT*44) $\vdash Fp \lor Op \lor Ip$ (Either p is forbidden or p is obligatory or p is indifferent)

$\quad$ Pf. (1) $\vdash p \supset p$ $\quad$ PL

$\quad$ (2) $\vdash (Pp \& P \sim p) \supset (Pp \& P \sim p)$ $\quad$ Sub. (1)

$\quad$ (3) $\vdash \sim Fp \& \sim Op . \supset Ip$ $\quad$ (2),(T5), (T2),(Dd3)

$\quad$ (4) $\vdash \sim (Fp \lor Op) \supset Ip$ $\quad$ (3),PL

$\quad$ (5) $\vdash Fp \lor Op \lor Ip$ $\quad$ (4),PL

(OT*45) $\vdash Ip \supset I \sim p$ (If p is indifferent, then not-p is also indifferent)

$\quad$ Pf. (1) $\vdash (Pp \& P \sim p) \supset (Pp \& P \sim p)$ $\quad$ PL

$\quad$ (2) $\vdash Ip \supset (P \sim \sim p \& P \sim p)$ $\quad$ (1),(Dd3), PL

$\quad$ (3) $\vdash Ip \supset (P \sim p \& P \sim \sim p)$ $\quad$ (2),PL

$\quad$ (4) $\vdash Ip \supset I \sim p$ $\quad$ (3),(Dd3)

Indeed, most of (OT*1) — (OT*40) are also variant the-

orems of FÅ. Despite the fact that FÅ shares many theorems of OT*, there are notable differences between these
two systems which deserve our attention. Among them, the
following are the most significant ones.

(1) It is no longer the case that a "tautologous-act"
is obligatory. Neither is it true that a "contradictory-act"
is forbidden. That is, the variant theorems (OT*17)′ and
(OT*18)′ below of (OT*17) and (OT*18) are not theorems
of FÅ.

(OT*17)′   OAaNa   (a-or-not-a is obligatory)

(OT*18)′   FKaNa   (a-and-not-a is forbidden)

This can be easily verified.

This feature may be looked upon by some deontic
logicians as a desirable feature.

(2) System FÅ like system vW contains no theorems
in which iterated modalities are involved. But unlike vW,
FÅ is not a variant subsystem of OT*. For instance, the
following rather counter-intuitive thesis (7.2) is a theorem
of FÅ.

(7.2)   (Pa & Pb) ⊃ PKab (If a is permissible and b is
             permissible then a-and-b is permissible)

However, its variant

(7.2)′   (Pp & Pq) ⊃ P (p & q)

is *not* a theorem of OT*. [6] Hence, (7.2) is not a theorem
of vW, either.

In addition to (7.2), system FÅ also contains other
counter-intuitive theorems. For instance

(7.3.)   Ia & Ib . ⊃ IKab (If a is indifferent and b is

---

[6] We defer the proof that (7.2)′ is not a theorem of OT* until the
end of section 9.

indifferent, then a-and-b is indifferent)

(3) Another significant difference between system FÅ and system OT* is that while the former has a finite characteristic matrix, [7] the latter does not have this property. To show that system OT* does not have a finite characteristic matrix, we first recall Dugundji's proof that there is no finite characteristic matrix for any one of Lewis systems. Now, his proof can be easily modified to show that system M of von Wright (which is system T of Feys) also has no finite characteristic matrix, and to show that system OT*, being a variant subsystem of system T, also lacks this property.

7 This has been shown by Åqvist, *ibid.*

§ 8. DEONTIC MODALITIES AND ITERATION OF MODALITIES

Exactly in parallel to the usual definition of alethic modalities, we may put down a definition of *deontic modalities* as follows. A deontic modality is a well-formed formula that is constructed in terms of a propositional variable, '∼' and 'O'. Or, more precisely, we may define a deontic modality recursively:

i) Any propositional variable is a deontic modality.

ii) If α is a deontic modality, then $\ulcorner\sim\alpha\urcorner$ and $\ulcorner O\alpha\urcorner$ are deontic modalities.

iii) Nothing else is a deontic modality.

A deontic modality will be said to be of *degree* k (k ≥ 0) if it contains k occurrences of 'O'. A deontic modality of degree zero is an *improper* modality; otherwise, a *proper* one.

In what follows we shall prove some theorems in which iterated (proper) modalities are involved. None of these theorems, as we indicated before, are theorems of vW* or FÅ, since they are not even wffs of those systems.

(OT*46) ⊢OOp⊃Op (If it is obligatory that p is obligatory, then p is obligatory; or, if p is obligatorily obligatory, then p is obligatory)

Pf. (1) ⊢O(Op⊃p)   (Ad7)

(2) ⊢OOp⊃Op   (1),(Ad4)

(OT*47)—(OT*49) below are immediate consequences of (OT*46) and (T1)—(T12).

(OT*47) $\vdash OFp \supset Fp$ (If p is obligatorily forbidden, then p is forbidden)

(OT*48) $\vdash FPp \supset Fp$ (If p is forbiddenly permissible, then p is forbidden; or if it is forbidden that p is permissible, then p is forbidden)

(OT*49) $\vdash FP\sim p \supset Op$ (If not-p is forbiddenly permissible, then p is obligatory)

It is easily felt that to read ⌜FPA⌝ as A is *forbiddenly permissible* seems extremely strange. But is it more strange than to read ⌜□◇A⌝ as A is necessarily possible?

The following theorem is another way to express what is said in (OT*47).

(OT*50) $\vdash O(Fp \supset \sim p)$ (It ought to be the case that if p is forbidden, then not-p is the case, or, then p is not done)
            Pf. (Ad7), PL, (T9)

(OT*51) $\vdash O(p \supset Pp)$ (It ought to be the case that if p is done then it is permissible)
            Pf. (OT*50), PL, (T5)

(OT*52) $\vdash Op \supset OPp$ (If p is obligatory, then p is obligatorily permissible)
            Pf. (OT*51), (Ad4), PL

(OT*53) $\vdash Fp \supset FOp$ (If p is forbidden, then p is forbiddenly obligatory). Another strange English rendering.
            Pf. (1) $\vdash Op \supset OPp$ (OT*52)
                (2) $\vdash O\sim p \supset OP\sim p$ Sub. (1)
                (3) $\vdash Fp \supset O\sim Op$ (2), (T9), (T2)
                (4) $\vdash Fp \supset FOp$ (3), (T9)

(OT*54) $\vdash PFp \supset P\sim p$ (If p is permissibly forbidden, then not-p is permissible)

Pf. (1) ⊢Op⊃OPp (OT*52)

(2) ⊢~OPp⊃~Op (1),PL

(3) ⊢P~Pp⊃P~p (2),(T2)

(4) ⊢PFp⊃P~p (3),(T5)

(OT*55) ⊢POp⊃Pp (If p is permissibly obligatory, then p is permissible)

pf. (1) ⊢Fp⊃FOp (OT*53)

(2) ⊢~FOp⊃~Fp (1),PL

(3) ⊢POp⊃Pp (2),(T5)

(OT*56) ⊢Pp⊃PPp (If p is permissible, then p is permissibly permissible)

Pf. (1) ⊢OOp⊃Op (OT*46)

(2) ⊢~Op⊃~OOp (1),PL

(3) ⊢~O~p⊃~OO~p Sub.(2)

(4) ⊢Pp⊃P~O~p (3), (T4),(T2)

(5) ⊢Pp⊃PPp (4),(T4)

In view of the rules (Rd4) and (Rd5), we know that we can establish theorems containing deontic modalities of greater and greater degree. For example, from (OT*56) by five applications of (Rd4), we have

(8.1)   ⊢OOOOOPp⊃OOOOOPPp

And then by three additional applications of (Rd5), we obtain

(8.2)   ⊢PPPOOOOOPp⊃PPPOOOOOPPp

which is an abbreviation of

(8.3)   ⊢~O~~O~~O~OOOOO~O~p⊃
                ~O~~O~~O~OOOOO~O~~O~p

which is equivalent to

(8.4) $\vdash\, \sim\!OOO\!\sim\!OOOOO\!\sim\!O\!\sim\!p \supset$
         $\sim\!OOO\!\sim\!OOOOO\!\sim\!OO\!\sim\!p$ [1]

Thus we have a theorem involving modalities of degree nine and degree ten, respectively.

Although the number of modalities can be multiplied indefinitely, we may, as in the case of alethic modal logic, ask the question: How many irreducible deontic modalities do we have in system OT*? The answer is easily obtained. It has infinitely many modalities.

To see this. First we recall the well-known result, due to Sobociński, [2] that system T possesses an infinite number of (alethic) modalities. Now, since system OT* is a deontic variant subsystem of T, it is obvious that OT* possesses at least as many deontic modalities as T contains alethic modalities. This follows from the fact that there can be no OT* theorems other than those whose variants already appeared in T that can be used to reduce the number of modalities. Therefore, system OT* possesses an infinite number of deontic modalities. As is easily seen, this infinity is of course denumerable.

---

1 We shall not try to render this formula into everyday language.
2 Sobociński, *ibid*.

§9. SYSTEM OS4* AND ITS FOURTEEN MODALITIES

System OS4*, as we know, is a system of deontic logic resulting by adding to system OT* the following axiom:

(Ad8)　⊢OP⊃OOp (If p is obligatory, then p is obliga-
　　　　torily obligatory)

Hence, every theorem of OT* is also a theorem of OS4*. Because of this relationship and in view of continuity, we shall let (OS4*1) — (OS4*56) denote the same theorems, respectively, as (OT*1) — (OT*56). Thus, the next theorem of OS4* will be (OS4*57).

(OS4*57)　⊢O∼p⊃OO∼p (If not-p is obligatory, then
　　　　it is obligatorily obligatory)
　　　　Pf. (Ad8), PL

Another way of expressing the same thing is this:

(9.1)　　　⊢Fp⊃OFp (If p is forbidden, then p is obliga-
　　　　torily forbidden)

which is the converse of (OT*48).

(OS4*58)　⊢O∼p≡OO∼p (Not-p is obligatory if and
　　　　only if it is obligatorily obligatory)
　　　　Pf. (OS4*57), (OT*46), PL

Another way of expressing this theorem is the follow-ing theorem.

(OS4*59)　⊢PPp≡Pp　(p is permissibly permissible if
　　　　and only if it is permissible)
　　　　Pf. (OS4*58), PL. (T2), (T4)

(OS4*60)　⊢OOp≡Op (p is obligatorily obligatory if and

only if it is obligatory)

Pf. (Ad8), (OT*46)

(OS4*61) ⊢O∼Op⊃∼Op (If p is obligatorily not obligatory then it is not obligatory)

Pf. (1) ⊢Op⊃OOp (Ad8)

(2) ⊢∼OOp⊃∼Op (1),PL

(3) ⊢P∼Op⊃P∼p (2),(T2)

(4) ⊢Op⊃Pp (OT*11)

(5) ⊢O∼Op⊃P∼Op Sub.(4)

(6) ⊢O∼Op⊃P∼p (3)(5), PL

(7) ⊢O∼Op⊃∼Op (6),(T2)

(OS4*62) ⊢O∼Op≡O∼O∼O∼Op (If p is obligatorily not obligatory, then p is obligatorily not obligatorily not obligatorily not obligatory)

Pf. (1) ⊢O∼Op⊃∼Op (OS4*61)

(2) ⊢PO∼Op⊃P∼Op (1),(Rd5)

(3) ⊢∼O∼O∼Op⊃∼O∼∼Op (2), (T4)

(4) ⊢∼O∼O∼Op⊃∼OOp (3),PL

(5) ⊢∼O∼O∼Op⊃∼Op (4), (OS4*60)

(6) ⊢O∼O∼O∼Op⊃O∼Op (5),(Rd4)

(7) ⊢Op⊃∼O∼Op (1), PL

(8) ⊢OOp⊃O∼O∼Op (7),(Rd4)

(9) ⊢Op⊃O∼O∼Op (8), (OS4*60)

(10) ⊢O∼Op⊃O∼O∼O∼Op Sub. (9)

(11) ⊢O∼Op≡O∼O∼O∼Op (6)(10), PL

Theorem (OS4*60) and (OS4*62) may be regarded as "reduction theorems" of system OS4*.

Since OS4* is a deontic subsystem of S4, it follows, by

the reasons we mentioned earlier, that OS4* contains at least as many deontic modalities as S4 contains alethic modalities. Hence, system OS4* possesses at least fourteen distinct deontic modalities. However, in the light of the above reduction theorems, we are able to show that OS4* possesses exactly fourteen distinct modalities. They are:

(9.2)   (1) p ⎫
                                              ⎬ degree 0—improper
        (2) $\sim p$ ⎭

        (3) Op ⎫
        (4) $O\sim p\,(Fp)$ ⎪
        (5) $\sim Op$ ⎬ degree 1
        (6) $O\sim p\,(Pp)$ ⎭

        (7) $O\sim Op\,(FOp)$ ⎫
        (8) $O\sim O\sim p\,(OPp)$ ⎪
        (9) $\sim O\sim Op\,(POp)$ ⎬ degree 2 ⎫ proper
        (10) $\sim O\sim O\sim p\,(PFp)$ ⎭   ⎬

        (11) $O\sim O\sim Op\,(OPOp)$ ⎫
        (12) $O\sim O\sim O\sim p\,(OPFp)$ ⎪
        (13) $\sim O\sim O\sim Op\,(PFOp)$ ⎬ degree 3
        (14) $\sim O\sim O\sim O\sim p\,(POPp)$ ⎭

These fourteen modalities are distinct. This follows from the well-known fact that the corresponding fourteen alethic modalities in S4 are distinct.

To show that (9.2) is a complete list of distinct (irreducible) deontic modalities in OS4*, let us, first of all, make the following observation:

(9.3)   (9.2) is a complete list of distinct irreducible deontic modalities (in OS4*) of degree equal to or less than three.

To prove this, let us consider four different cases:

(Case 1) Modalities of degree zero. That is, a propositional variable prefixed by a string of '∼''s of any length. (Other candidates will turn out to be either not deontic modalities or not of degree zero). In this case, (1) and (2) of (9.2) can be seen to constitute a complete list in view of the following elementary logical laws:

(9.4) $\lceil \overbrace{\sim \cdots \cdots \sim}^{2k} \alpha \rceil \equiv \alpha$

(9.5) $\lceil \overbrace{\sim \cdots \cdots \sim}^{2k+1} \alpha \rceil \equiv \lceil \sim \alpha \rceil$

(Case 2) Modalities of degree one. That is, a modality in which there is exactly one occurrence of 'O' prefixed or suffixed by a string of '∼''s (maybe an empty string) and followed by a propositional variable. Or, in short, a modality of the following form:

(9.6)   ···O---p

where '···' and '---' are strings (maybe empty) of '∼''s. Again, by (9.4) and (9.5), it is easily seen that (3) — (6) in (9.2) exhaust all the possibilities of distinct deontic modalities of degree one.

(Case 3) Modalities of degree two. That is, a modality with two occurrences of 'O''s each of which may be pre- fixed or suffixed by a string (perhaps empty) of '∼''s and finally followed by a propositional variable. In other words, modalities of the following form:

(9.7)   ···O---O—··—p

Suppose that the number of '∼''s in the string be- tween the two occurrences of 'O''s is even, then, by (9.4) and PL, (9.7) becomes

(9.8)   ···OO—··—p

which by (OS4*60) is the same as

(9.10) $\cdots O - \bullet \bullet - p$

That is to say, in this case, (9.6) is reduced to a modality of a lesser degree. Hence, we need only consider the case in which there is a string of odd number of '$\sim$''s between 'O''s. But this, by (9.5) means that we need only to consider modalities of the following form:

(9.11) $\cdots O \sim O - \bullet \bullet - p$

Again, by (9.4) and (9.5), it is easily seen that $(7) - (9)$ in (9.2) are the only distinct modalities of degree two.

(Case 4) Modalities of degree three. The proof is exactly analogous to the proof in (Case 3) except here we need to consider modalities of the following form:

(9.12) $\cdots O \sim O \sim O - - - p$

Again, $(11) - (14)$ of (9.2) exhaust all the possibilities. This concludes the proof that (9.2) is a complete list of distinct deontic modalities of degree equal to or less than three.

We now turn to the following thesis:

(9.12)   There are no irreducible deontic modalities (in OS4*) of degree greater than three.

We shall prove this thesis by verifying the following claim. If M is a modality of degree equal to or greater than three, then M is equivalent, i. e., reducible, to one of the fourteen modalities in (9.2). The proof is carried out by mathematical induction on the degree of M. When the degree of M is four, then, for the reason we indicated and proved above, we only need to consider the following four cases:

   i) $M = O \sim O \sim O \sim Op$

   ii) $M = O \sim O \sim O \sim O \sim p$

   iii) $M = \sim O \sim O \sim O \sim Op$

iv) $M = \sim O \sim O \sim O \sim O \sim p$

But these modalities, by (OS4*62), are, respectively, the same as

v) $O \sim Op$

vi) $O \sim O \sim p$

vii) $\sim O \sim Op$

viii) $\sim O \sim O \sim p$

which are, in fact, (7), (8), (9) and (10) of (9.2), respectively. Hence, they are not new modalities. And our thesis holds for the base of the induction.

Now, as the hypothesis of the induction, suppose that our thesis is true when the degree of M is k (k≥4), we want to show that our thesis is still true when the degree of M is k+1. Four cases to be considered (other cases are dismissed for the same reason stated above):

i) $M = OM'$

ii) $M = \sim OM'$

iii) $M = O \sim M'$

iv) $M = \sim O \sim M'$

where M′ is a modality of degree k and thus, by the hypothesis, can be reduced to one of the fourteen modalities of (9.2). Again, by (9.4), (9.5), (OS4*60), (OS4*62) and PL, and by checking through each of the fourteen possibilities for M′, we will see that in each case M turns out to be equivalent to one of (1)—(14) in (9.2). Therefore, by the principle of mathematical induction, we conclude that there are no modalities of degree greater than three which cannot be reduced to one of the fourteen modalities in (9.2).

Next, by combining (9.3) and (9.12) we obtain immediatly the result that (9.2) is a complete list of irreducible deontic modalities in OS4*. That is to say, system OS4*, just as system S4, possesses exactly fourteen irreducible modalities.

The implication relations holding among the deontic modalities are again exactly parallel to those holding among their corresponding alethic modalities. They can be summarized in the following chart: [1]

$$Op \Rightarrow O \sim O \sim Op \Rightarrow \begin{Bmatrix} \sim O \sim Op \\ O \sim O \sim p \end{Bmatrix} \Rightarrow \sim O \sim O \sim O \sim p \Rightarrow \sim O \sim p$$

where '$\Rightarrow$' denotes logical implication. [2]

From this chart, we can draw some further theorems of OS4* which have not yet appeared above. However, we will not do so here.

Before closing this section, let us prove a claim we made in a note, i.e., note 6, of section 7. That is, we want to show that

(7.2)′   Pp & Pq . $\supset$ P(p & q)

is *not* a theorem of OT*.

Let us prove this by showing a stronger result: that (7.2)′ is not even a theorem of OS4*. And since OS4* is a supersystem of OT*, the desired result follows.

The proof is as follows. Suppose, for a contradiction, that (7.2)′ *were* a theorem of OS4*, then we could establish the following:

(1) $\vdash$ Pp & Pq . $\equiv$ P(p & q)   (7.2)′, (OS4*31)

(2) $\vdash \sim$ (Pp & Pq) $\equiv \sim$ P(p & q)   (1),PL

(3) $\vdash \sim$ (Pp & P$\sim$p) $\equiv \sim$ P(p & p)   Sub.(2)

(4) $\vdash \sim$ (Pp & P$\sim$p) $\equiv$ F(p & $\sim$p)   (3),(T6),PL

(5) $\vdash$ F(p & $\sim$p) $\supset$. $\sim$Pp v $\sim$P$\sim$p   (4),PL

---

1 Cf. Feys [1965], p. 95.

2 The improper modalities are not among them, because (A5) fails in deontic logic.

(6) $\vdash F(p \& \sim q)$ (OS4*18)
(7) $\vdash \sim Pp \lor \sim P \sim p$ (5) (6), PL
(8) $\vdash Pp \supset Op$ (7), PL, (T1)
(9) $\vdash Op \supset Pp$ (OS4*11)
(10) $\vdash Op \equiv Pp$ (8), (9), PL
(11) $\vdash Op \equiv \sim P \sim p$ (OS4*1)
(12) $\vdash Op \equiv \sim O \sim p$ (10)(11), PL

And since '$Op \equiv \sim O \sim p$' is provable, it follows together with (OS4*60) that the fourteen modalities of OS4* reduce to six. But this is absurd, because we know that OS4* possesses at least fourteen modalities. Hence, we have a contradiction. That means (7.2)′ ca*nnot* be a theorem in OS4*. A similar proof can be used to show that (7.2)′ is not a theorem of OS5*, either. [3]

---

[3] Another way of obtaining the same result is by showing that the deontic variant of (7.2)′, namely, '$\Diamond p \& \Diamond q . \supset \Diamond (p \& q)$,' is not a theorem of S5.

§ 10. SYSTEM OS5* AND ITS
SIX MODALITIES

Next comes the strongest of our deontic systems, OS5*, which is the result of adding (Ad9), i.e.,

$$\sim Op \supset O \sim Op$$

as an axiom to OS4* above. Thus, every theorem of OS4* is a theorem of OS5*. And again we will denote by '(OS5*1)'—'(OS5*62)' the theorems (OS4*1)—(OS4*62), respectively.

The following is an additional theorem of OS5*:

(OS5*63) $\vdash O \sim Op \equiv \sim Op$ (p is obligatorily not obligatory if and only if p is not obligatory)

Pf. (OS5*61), (Ad9)

This is the reduction theorem of OS5*. In view of it, the fourteen modalities in OS4* are immediately reduced to the following six:

(10.1)   (1) p   (2) $\sim p$

          (3) Op   (4) $O \sim p$ (Fp)

          (5) $\sim Op$ (6) $\sim O \sim p$ (Pp)

The only implication relation holding among these modalities is depicted by (Ad6), or equivalently, by (OS5*11).

§ 11. ANDERSONIAN CONSTANT AND DEONTIC SYSTEMS OM, OM′, OM″

Instead of following the manner in which we con-structed the deontic logics OT*, OS4* and OS5*, Anderson [1956] took three systems of alethic modal logic M, M′ and M″ of von Wright—which are equivalent, respectively, to T of Feys, S4 and S5 of Lewis—let them remain intact, but added to the vocabulary of each system a propositional constant '$\mathscr{B}$'. He then defined the notions of obligation, permission and forbiddance in terms of this constant. The results turn out to be three deontic logics, OM, OM′ and OM″.

To reconstruct these three systems, let us, first of all, put down the primitive basis of the weakest one, that is, system OM.

I. Vocabulary
  i) Propositional variables: 'p', 'q', 'r', 'p₁'...
  ii) Propositional constant: '$\mathscr{B}$'
  iii) Sentential connectives: '∼', '&', 'v', '⊃', '≡', '◇'
  iv) Grouping indicators: '[', ']'

II. Formation rules
  i) A propositional variable or a propositional constant standing alone is a wff.
  ii) If A and B are wffs, so are ⌜∼A⌝, ⌜◇A⌝, ⌜[A & B]⌝, ⌜[AvB]⌝, ⌜[A⊃B]⌝, and ⌜[A≡B]⌝.
  iii) Nothing else is a wff.

III. Axioms

(A1) ⎫
(A2) ⎬ (Same)
(A3) ⎭

(AN4) $\vdash p \supset \Diamond p$

(AN5) $\vdash \Diamond [p \lor q] \equiv [\Diamond p \lor \Diamond q]$

IV. Rules of inference

(R1) ⎫
      ⎬ (Same)
(R2) ⎭

(RN3) Extensionality: From $\ulcorner A \supset B \urcorner$ we may infer $\ulcorner \Diamond A \supset \Diamond B \urcorner$.[1]

(RN4) Necessitation: From A we may infer $\ulcorner \sim \Diamond \sim A \urcorner$.

V. Definitions

(DN1) $\ulcorner \Box A \urcorner =_{Df} \ulcorner \sim \Diamond \sim A \urcorner$

(DN2) $\ulcorner A \dashv B \urcorner =_{Df} \ulcorner \Box [A \supset B] \urcorner$

(DN3) $\mathscr{S} =_{Df} \text{'} \mathscr{B} \& \Diamond \sim \mathscr{B} \text{'}$

(DN4) $\ulcorner PA \urcorner =_{Df} \ulcorner \Diamond [A \& \sim \mathscr{S}] \urcorner$

(DN5) $\ulcorner OA \urcorner =_{Df} \ulcorner \sim P \sim A \urcorner$

(DN6) $\ulcorner FA \urcorner =_{Df} \ulcorner \sim PA \urcorner$

(DN7) $\ulcorner IA \urcorner =_{Df} \ulcorner PA \& P \sim A \urcorner$[2]

System OM' is the result of adding the following (AN6) to OM.

(AN6) $\vdash \Diamond \Diamond p \supset \Diamond p$

---

1 This is stronger than von Wright's original version, see von Wright [1951b], p. 85.

2 $\ulcorner IA \urcorner$ is not defined in Anderson, *ibid.*, but we add it here for completeness.

And if we add (AN7) to OM′, we have system OM″.

(AN7) $\vdash \Diamond \sim \Diamond p \supset \sim \Diamond p$ [3]

Intuitively speaking, '$\mathscr{B}$' stands for some unspecified bad thing, and '$\mathscr{S}$' denotes "sanction" of a certain kind which is defined as "the bad thing that can be avoided happens" ('$\mathscr{B} \& \Diamond \mathscr{B}$'). And the permissibility of bringing it about that A is defined as "A can be done without the sanction" ('$\Diamond [A \& \sim \mathscr{S}]$').

Thus, in Andersonian systems, we are not reading '$\square$' as obligatory and '$\Diamond$' as permissible. When we say, for example, that

(OT*56) $Pp \supset PPp$

is provable in OM, what we mean is that there is a proof of

(11.1) $\Diamond [p \& \sim \mathscr{S}] \supset \Diamond [\Diamond [p \& \sim \mathscr{S}] \& \sim \mathscr{S}]$ [4]

In what follows we shall make free use of any theorem which has already been established in Anderson [1956]. No proofs in this case will be given, and the theorem numbering prefixed by 'OM', 'OM″' or 'OM″' is Anderson's.

---

[3] (AN6) and (AN7) are called by von Wright "the first reduction axiom" and "the second reduction axiom", respectively. See, *ibid.*, p. 84.

[4] For a proof of (11. 1), see Anderson, *ibid.*, p. 188.

§ 12. THE RELATION BETWEEN
OT*, OS4*, OS5* AND OM, OM′, OM″

It turns out that OT*, OS4* and OS5* bear a certain relation, respectively, to OM, OM′ and OM″. Namely, that every theorem of OT* (OS4* or OS5*) is an abbreviation of a certain theorem of OM (OM′ or OM″). That is to say, the former are quasi-subsystems of the latter. We shall also say that the latter quasi-contain the former.

To make a careful distinction between a theorem and an abbreviation of a theorem is all-important when inter-system inquiry is under way. This is especially the case when different systems under consideration possess different symbols. For example, we may ask the question: whether or not the following (OM8) is a theorem of OT*?

(OM8) $\vdash Pp \supset \diamond [p \ \& \sim \mathscr{S}]$

The answer cannot be given as easily as one might expect. In one sense, (OM8) *is* a theorem of OT*, because one might say that it is nothing but

(12.1) $Pp \supset Pp$

having in mind that (OM8) can be abbreviated as (12.1). However, in another equally, if not more significant, sense, (OM8) is *not* a theorem of OT*. Indeed, it is not even a well-formed formula of OT*.

If we are willing to take the relation of quasi-containing seriously, we may show that OT*, OS4* and OS5* are quasi-contained, respectively, by OM, OM′ and OM″. To see this, we shall first show that OT* is a quasi-subsystem of OM. In order to prove this, it suffices to demonstrate that all axioms of OT* are either axioms or theorems, or their abbreviations, of OM, and that every rule of OT* is either a rule or a derived rule of OM.

The axioms (A1) —(A3) are the same. (Ad4), (Ad6) and (Ad7) can be proved in OM as follows (as we have said above, we shall make use of the theorems already established in OM).

(Ad4)　$\vdash O\,(p\supset q)\supset(Op\supset Oq)$

　　　Pf.　(1)　$\vdash (Op\ \&\ O\,(p\supset q))\supset Oq$　(OM29)

　　　　　(2)　$\vdash O\,(p\supset q)\supset(Op\supset Oq)$　(1), PL

(Ad6)　$\vdash Op\supset\sim O\sim p$

　　　Pf.　(1)　$\vdash Op\supset Pp$　(OM10)

　　　　　(2)　$\vdash Pp\equiv\sim O\sim p$　(OM5)

　　　　　(3)　$\vdash Op\supset\sim O\sim p$　(1)(2), PL

(AD7)　$\vdash O\,(Op\supset p)$

　　　Pf.　(1)　$\vdash O\,(Op\supset p)$　(OM45)

Again, the rules (R1)—(R2) are the same. It suffices to show that (Rd3), from A to infer $\ulcorner OA\urcorner$, is a derived rule in OM.

The proof is as follows. Suppose A is a theorem (or axiom) of OM, we want to show that from this it follows that $\ulcorner OA\urcorner$, or rather, its abbreviation, is also a theorem of OM. We may establish the proof as follows:

　　Pf.　(1)　$\vdash p\supset(\sim p\supset q)$　PL

　　　　(2)　$\vdash A\supset(\sim A\supset\mathscr{S})$　Sub. (1)

　　　　(3)　$\vdash\sim(\sim A\supset\mathscr{S})\supset\sim A$　(2), PL

　　　　(4)　$\vdash\diamondsuit\sim(\sim A\supset\mathscr{S})\supset\diamondsuit\sim A$　(3), (RN3)

　　　　(5)　$\vdash\sim\diamondsuit\sim A\supset\sim\diamondsuit\sim(\sim A\supset\mathscr{S})$　(4), PL

　　　　(6)　$\vdash A$　Assumption

　　　　(7)　$\vdash\sim\diamondsuit\sim A$　(6), (RN4)

(8) $\vdash \sim \diamond \sim (\sim A \supset \mathscr{S})$ (5) (7), (R2)

(9) $\vdash \sim \diamond (\sim A \& \sim \mathscr{S})$ (8), PL

(10) $\vdash \sim P \sim A$ (9), (DN4)

(11) $\vdash OA$ (10), (DN5)

This completes the proof that OT* is a quasi-subsystem of OM.

To show that OS4 is a quasi-subsystem of OM′, we need only to show that (Ad8) of OS4 is provable in OM′. The proof:

(Ad8) $\vdash Op \supset OOp$

Pf.   (1) $\vdash PPp \supset Pp$ (OM′60)

(2) $\vdash PP \sim p \supset P \sim p$ Sub. (1)

(3) $\vdash \sim P \sim p \supset \sim PP \sim p$ (2), PL

(4) $\vdash Op \equiv \sim P \sim p$ (OM1)

(5) $\vdash Op \supset FP \sim p$ (3) (4), PL, (DN6)

(6) $\vdash Fp \equiv O \sim p$ (OM4)

(7) $\vdash Op \supset O \sim P \sim p$ (5) (6), PL

(8) $\vdash Op \supset OOp$ (7) (4), PL

And to show that OS5* is a quasi-subsystem of OM″, we prove that (Ad9) of OS5* is an (abbreviated) theorem of OM″.

(Ad9) $\vdash \sim Op \supset O \sim Op$

Pf.   (1) $\vdash P \sim Pp \equiv \sim Pp$ (OM″64)

(2) $\vdash P \sim Pp \supset \sim Pp$ (1), PL

(3) $\vdash P \sim P \sim p \supset \sim P \sim p$ Sub. (2)

(4) $\vdash Op \equiv \sim P \sim p$ (OM1)

(5) $\vdash POp \supset Op$ (3) (4), PL

(6) $\vdash \sim Op \supset \sim POp$ (5), PL

(7) $\vdash \sim Op \supset FOp$ (6), (DN6)

(8) $\vdash Fp \equiv O \sim p$ (OM4)

(9) $\vdash \sim Op \supset O \sim Op$ (7) (8), PL

This concludes our proof that OT*, OS4* and OS5* are, respectively, quasi-subsystems of OM, OM′ and OM″.

The following chart shows the containing relations holding among the systems we have so far discussed. We make no effort to distinguish between containing, quasi-containing, or the containing with respect to a certain variation of symbols, as the distinctions are now quite obvious. The broken line shows that the two systems connected by it share some theorems but neither contains or is contained by the other.

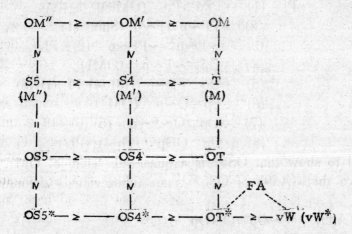

Of course, it goes without saying that the containing relation is, among other things, reflexive, transitive but nonsymmetric.

§ 13. FURTHER THEOREMS AND FURTHER PROBLEMS IN OM—OM″, KANTIAN PRINCIPLE AND THE PARADOX OF THE GOOD SAMARITAN

The interest of the Andersonian approach to deontic logic lies mainly in the simplicity of constructing deontic modalities. Thus, in system OM—OM″ we are able not only to present deontic concepts but also to express alethic modal concepts. Moreover, we can systematize these two groups of concepts in combination. That is to say, we will have well-formed formulas of OM—OM″ in which both deontic and alethic modalities appear. This feature is interesting because it seems clear that alethic concepts do find a way into our moral discussion. For instance, someone may want to follow Kant in saying that what is obligatory must be possible. ("ought" implies "can"). And here "possible" or "can" is clearly an alethic modal concept.

However, this great gain has not been made with no pains. As is too familiar in philosophy, when we widen the deontic horizon by allowing the alethic modalities, some additional problems immediately develop themselves in the newly acquired territory.

In what follows, we shall present some of the interesting deontic theorems which are provable in OM (hence, in OM′ and OM″) but not in OS5* (hence, not in OS4*, nor in OT* and vW*). Most of them are theorems in which both deontic and alethic modalities present themselves.

(OM7) $\vdash Op \equiv . \sim p \dashv 3 \mathscr{S}$ (p is obligatory if and only if not-p strictly implies the sanction) [1]

(OM21) $\vdash \Box p \supset Op$ (If p is necessary, then p is obligatory)

(OM23) $\vdash \sim \Diamond p \supset Fp$ (If p is impossible, then p is forbidden)

These two theorems state something stronger than what are expressed in (OT*17) and (OT*18). According to (OM21) and (OM23), for instance, not only that to go and not to go to fight in Vietnam is forbidden, it is also forbidden to draw a round square or to trisect an arbitrary angle with only a ruler and a compass.

(OM24) $\vdash Op \supset \Diamond p$ (If p is obligatory, then p is possible)

This is the so-called Kantian principle that what one ought to do one can do. But is this a sound principle?

As we recall, the formulation of commitment in terms of obligation and the conditional leads to paradoxical results. Now, in OM—OM″, we may want to propose another candidate for that concept, we might want to let strict implication together with obligation capture the essential idea of commitment. That is, we may want to read 'p∢3Oq' as "p commits us to do q".

Under this new formulation, the paradoxes of derived obligation disappear. Because the following are no longer theorems of OM—OM″.

(13.1) $Fp \supset . p \dashv 3 Oq$

---

[1] Anderson [1956] read '∢3' as logical entailment. Later in [1967] he preferred "relevant implication".

(13.2) $\quad Op \supset . \; q \dashv 3 Op$

However, it seems questionable whether people want to make moral commitment as strong as a strict implication.

The following theorems are also of special interest:

(OM27) $\quad [Pp \,\&. \; p \dashv 3 q] \supset Pq$ (If p is permissible and p strictly implies q, then q is permissible)

(OM28) $\quad [Fp \,\&. \; q \dashv 3 p] \supset Fq$ (If p is forbidden and q strictly implies p, then q is forbidden)

Now, if we follow Anderson to read '$\dashv 3$' as entailment, another "paradox" follows from (OM28). Consider the following situation. Suppose that robbery is forbidden. Since to help someone who is the victim of robbery entails, among other things, that robbery occurs, it follows, by (OM28), that the good Samaritan who helps the man who becomes the victim of robbery on his way to Jericho also does something forbidden. This unhappy result is called *the paradox of the Good Samaritan.*

§ 14. VON WRIGHT'S
TENSE-DEONTIC SYSTEMS

In §5 we indicated that von Wright proposed one type of deontic logic which may be called *tense-deontic logic*. It is a kind of deontic logic that is based upon a certain system of tense logic. But since von Wright has outlined several different systems of tense logic, [1] we may have several different systems of tense-deontic logic.

In this section we shall briefly explain what a tense-deontic logic (of von Wright's type) is and indicate the advantage of this kind of deontic logic.

First of all, we shall reconstruct here a system of von Wright's tense logic which we shall call system vW. This system may be regarded as a formalization of our intuitive tense connective 'α and then β' as in "The door of Rm 14 Morrill Hall is open *and then* the door of Rm 14 Morrill Hall is closed" where 'α' and 'β' stand for the propositions that the door of Rm 14 Morrill Hall is open and that the door of Rm 14 Morrill Hall is closed, respectively. We shall symbolize this binary tense connective as '$\alpha \rangle\!\!\rightarrow \beta$'. [2]

The following is an axiomatization of von Wright's system vW. [3]

---

1 See von Wright [1965b] and [1966].
2 Von Wright symbolizes 'α and then β' as '$\alpha T\beta$'. See von Wright, *ibid*.
3 Cf. von Wright [1966].

I. Vocabulary
   i) Propositional variables: 'p', 'q', 'r', 'p₁',...
   ii) Propositional connectives: '$\sim$', '&', 'v', '$\supset$', '$\equiv$', '$\rightarrowtail$'. (The first five are the usual truth-functional connectives, the last one is the tense connective 'and then')
   iii) Grouping indicators: '[', ']'.

II. Formation rules
   i) A propositional variable standing alone is a wff (We shall call it a *tense*-wff or T-wff).
   ii) If A and B are (T-)wffs, so are $\ulcorner \sim A \urcorner$, $\ulcorner [A \& B] \urcorner$, $\ulcorner [AvB] \urcorner$, $\ulcorner [A \supset B] \urcorner$, $\ulcorner [A \equiv B] \urcorner$ and $\ulcorner [A \rightarrowtail B] \urcorner$. [4]
   iii) Nothing else is a (T-)wff.

III. Axioms
   (A1) — (A3)   Same as in system OT.
   (T4) $\vdash [p \vee q] \rightarrowtail [r \vee p_1] . \equiv [p \rightarrowtail r] \vee [p \rightarrowtail p_1] \vee [q \rightarrowtail r] \vee [q \rightarrowtail p_1]$
   (T5) $\vdash [p \rightarrowtail q] \& [r \rightarrowtail p_1] \equiv . [[p \& r] \rightarrowtail [q \& p_1] \vee [q \rightarrowtail p_1] \vee [p_1 \rightarrowtail q]]$
   (T6) $\vdash p \equiv [p \rightarrowtail [q \vee \sim q]]$
   (T7) $\vdash \sim [p \rightarrowtail [q \& \sim q]]$

IV. Rules of inference [5]
   (R1)   Substitution

---

[4] We rank these connectives as follows: '$\sim$', '&', 'v', '$\supset$', '$\equiv$', '$\rightarrowtail$' where a connective overranks (but is not overranked by) those standing on its left.

[5] Von Wright adds a rule which he calls the "rule of extensionality" to the following effect: "...that provably equivalent T-expressions [T-wffs] are interchangeable *salva veritate*". However, we shall not add this rule here, because the rule seems helpful only when we try, as von Wright does, to explore the semantical problems of system vWₜ.

(R2)   *modus ponens*

It may be noted that certain uses of the usual "temporal quantifiers" such as 'always', 'sometimes' and 'never' can be defined in terms of the tense connective '$\succ\!\!\rightarrow$' together with the usual propositional connectives. This has been shown by von Wright in [1966]. For instance, the sentence

(14.1)   The sun [now] rises in the east and will *always* rise in the east.

can be paraphrased as

(14.2)   The sun [now] rises in the east and it is not the case that whatever the circumstances may be, *and then* the sun does not rise in the east.

or in symbols

(14.3) $p \,\&\sim [(q \vee \sim q) \succ\!\!\rightarrow \sim p]$

where 'p' stands for 'The sun rises in the east' and 'q v ~q' depicts a condition or a state of affairs which is ever present. Let us use '$\oplus$' to mean 'always' in the above-mentioned sense, namely, '$\oplus$p' means 'It is the case that p now and it will be the case that p at all later times'. Then the following definition may be given:

(D14.1) $\ulcorner \oplus A \urcorner =_{\mathrm{Df}} \ulcorner A \,\&\sim (t \succ\!\!\rightarrow \sim A) \urcorner$

where 't' is a tautology in PL.

We are of course aware that 'always' is often used in a more extensive sense. 'It is always the case that p' usually means that it was the case that p and it is the case that p and it will be the case that p. Hence, we may say that '$\oplus$p' captures only a partial meaning of the commonsensical 'always', namely 'now and hereafter' or 'from now on'. But this partial meaning is of special interest to a deontic or imperative logician, because when we utter a command in which 'always' appears, the 'always' is used, as a rule, in the above less extensive sense. For instance, when we order:

(14.4)   Always keep the door closed!

we usually mean

(14.5)   Keep the door closed now and keep the door closed at all later times!

Hence 'ϕ' corresponds very closely to the use of 'always' in the usual deontic and/or imperative contexts. [6]

Likewise, 'sometimes' and 'never' also have corresponding less extensive meanings. We can always make the qualification "from now on" in their meanings.

If we say

(14.6)   Sometimes [now or at a later time] the sun does not rise in the east.

this presumably is the contradiction of (14.3). Thus, (14.6) can be symbolized as

$$\sim (p \& \sim ((q \lor \sim q) \rightarrowtail \sim p))$$

that is

(14.7) $\sim p \lor ((q \lor \sim q) \rightarrowtail \sim p)$

It follows that

(14.8)   Sometimes the sun rises in the east.

can be symbolized as

(14.9) $p \lor ((q \lor \sim q) \rightarrowtail p)$

If we use '$\odot$' to mean 'sometimes', then we have the following definition:

(D14.2) $\ulcorner \odot A \urcorner \underset{Df}{} \ulcorner \sim \phi \sim A \urcorner$

Again, '$\odot$' represents only a partial meaning of the every-

---

6 But we do not claim that past-tense commands are impossible. We leave the possibility open.

day use of 'sometimes'.

The meaning of 'never' can be likewise explained. When we say

(14.10)   The sun never rises in the east.

we mean

(14.11)   It is always the case that the sun does not rise in the east.

or

(14.12) $\phi \sim p$

that is

(14.13) $\sim p \,\&\sim (t \!\!>\!\!\longrightarrow\! p)$

Let us use '$\chi\!\!\!\!\!\;$' to mean 'never' in this sense, then we have the following definition:

(D14.3) $\ulcorner \chi\!\!\!\!\;A \urcorner =_{\mathrm{Df}} \ulcorner \phi \sim A \urcorner$

In what follows we shall list some of the theorems of system vW_t. We shall omit the proofs. Most of the theorems listed here coincide with the theorems given by von Wright, and the proofs can be found in von Wright [1966].

(Thm 1) $\vdash (p \!\!>\!\!\longrightarrow\! q) \lor (p \!\!>\!\!\longrightarrow\! \sim q) \lor (\sim p \!\!>\!\!\longrightarrow\! q) \lor (\sim p \!\!>\!\!\longrightarrow\! \sim q)$ (It is the case that p and then q, or it is the case that p and then not-q, or it is the case that not-p and then q, or it is the case that not-p and then not-q)

(Thm 2) $\vdash (p \!\!>\!\!\longrightarrow\! q) \supset p$ (If it is the case that (p and then q), then it is the case that p)

(Thm 3) $\vdash \sim ((p \,\&\sim p) \!\!>\!\!\longrightarrow\! q)$ (It is not the case that (it is the case that (p and not-p) and then q))

(Thm 4) $\vdash (p \,\&\, (q \!\!>\!\!\longrightarrow\! r)) \equiv ((p \,\&\, q) \!\!>\!\!\longrightarrow\! r)$

(Thm 5) $\vdash ((p \,\&\, q) \!\!>\!\!\longrightarrow\! r)) \supset (p \!\!>\!\!\longrightarrow\! r)$

(Thm 6) $\vdash (p \!\!>\!\!\longrightarrow\! (q \,\&\, r)) \supset (p \!\!>\!\!\longrightarrow\! q)$

(Thm 7) $\vdash ((p \rangle\!\!\rightarrow q) \,\&\, (p \rangle\!\!\rightarrow r)) \equiv ((p \rangle\!\!\rightarrow q) \rangle\!\!\rightarrow r)$

(Thm 8) $\vdash (p \rangle\!\!\rightarrow (q \rangle\!\!\rightarrow r)) \supset (p \rangle\!\!\rightarrow r)$

(Thm 9) $\vdash \oplus t$ (It is always the case that t)

(Thm 10) $\vdash \otimes f$ (It is never the case that f)

(Thm 11) $\vdash \oplus p \supset p$ (If it is always the case that p, then it is the case that p)

(Thm 12) $\vdash p \supset \odot p$ (If it is the case that p, then it is sometimes the case that p)

(Thm 13) $\vdash \oplus (p \,\&\, q) \equiv . \oplus p \,\&\, \oplus q$ (It is always the case that p-and-q if and only if it is always the case that p and it is always the case that q)

(Thm 15) $\vdash \otimes (p \vee q) \equiv . \otimes p \,\&\, \otimes q$ (Similarly)

(Thm 16) $\vdash \odot (p \vee q) \equiv . \odot p \vee \odot q$

(Thm 17) $\vdash \odot p \supset \sim \otimes p$ (If it is sometimes the case that p, then it is not the case that it is never the case that p)

The following theorems involve the iteration of temporal quantifiers:

(Thm 18) $\vdash \oplus p \supset \oplus \oplus p$ (If it is always the case that p, then it is always the case that it is always the case that p)

(Thm 19) $\vdash \odot \oplus p \supset \oplus \odot p$ (If it is sometimes the case that it is always the case that p, then it is always the case that it is sometimes the case that p)

Here we sense an unnaturalness or, rather, an unfamiliarity in the English renderings of '$\oplus \oplus p$', '$\odot \oplus p$' and '$\oplus \odot p$'. Tense logic like most other branches of logic goes beyond the scope of our bare intuition.

Let us now indicate how to extend the tense logical

system vW_t to a tense-deontic system. There are many ways to accomplish this goal. We shall however give only an example.

Suppose we add to the primitive basis of vW_t the following ingredients, the resulting system will be called a tense-deontic system $OT^*(vW_t)$.

First, to the vocabulary of vW_t, we add

I.   iv) Deontic operator: 'O'

Secondly, to the formation rules of vW_t we add

II.   iv) A T-wff is a wff.

     v) If A and B are wffs, so are ⌐OA⌐, ⌐~A⌐, ⌐[A & B]⌐, ⌐[A v B]⌐, ⌐[A ⊃ B]⌐ and ⌐[A≡B]⌐.

     vi) Nothing else is a wff.

Thirdly, we add the following axioms:

III. (Ad4)   ⊢O[p⊃q]⊃[Op⊃Oq]

     (Ad6)   ⊢Op⊃ ~O~p

     (Ad7)   ⊢O[Op⊃p]

And finally, to the rules of inference, we add

IV.   (Rd3)   Deontic necessitation.

It is immediately seen that the system $OT^*(vW_t)$ just constructed is, as the name suggests, a "combination" of our earlier (deontic) system OT^* and tense system vW_t. We may in the same manner combine vW_t with $OS4^*$ and obtain a tense-deontic system $OS4^*(vW)$, and so on.

One of the leading characteristics of this type of tense-deontic logic is that the deontic operator may take tense expressions (T-wffs) as its operands. This is a feature which is interesting enough to receive our closer attention, because it helps us, among other things, make precise what is the exact content of an obligation, an imperative, and what not. Let us first give an example to illustrate this point.

If a certain Mr. A gives Mr. B the following command:

(14.14)   Open the door!

Suppose further that the door is already open. Then Mr. B need not do anything in order to fulfill the command. The order is automatically carried out. Only in the case that the door is closed should Mr. B make the necessary effort of opening it to accomplish the command given by Mr. A in (14.14). However, these two different cases—in one of which Mr. B needs to make a genuine effort and in the other he does not need to—are not distinguished when (14.14) is uttered. But suppose the command is issued in the following manner:

(14.15)   Bring it about that (the door is closed and then the door is open)!

Then the order is clear. If the door is closed now, (14.15) simply orders one to open it. Suppose, on the other hand, that the door is open now, (14.15) orders one to first close it and then open it. In both cases, genuine efforts are demanded in order to fulfill the command in question.

Similar remarks can be made about the deontic "counterpart" [7] of (14.14). For instance, corresponding to (14.14) we may put down a deontic sentence like:

(14.16) Op

where 'p' stands for 'The door is open', and corresponding to (14.15) the following one:

(14.17) $O(q \rangle\!\!\rightarrow p)$

where 'q' stands for 'The door is closed'.

Likewise one may issue a command to the following effect:

---

[7] For the meaning of 'deontic counterpart', see § 24.

Keep the door open!

This may be symbolized in its deontic counterpart as

(14.18) $O \phi p$

These examples indicate that when we let the deontic operator apply to tense-wffs, we might make commands or obligations, and so on, more precisely stated. We could be more sure what is the exact content of a command, and hence what constitutes the fulfillment of that command.

However, only to let the tense wffs be candidates for the operands of a deontic operator seems not sufficient to cope with the problem we just pointed out. For example, suppose we say:

(14.19) $O(p \succ\!\!\!\to r)$

where 'p' stands for the same sentence as above, and 'r' stands for 'The light comes in'. That is, (14.19) means:

(14.20)   It ought to be the case that (the door is open and then the light comes in).

Now, suppose the opening of the door "naturally" brings in the light, then in order to fulfill (14.19), one need only open the door (if it is not already open). One need not do anything else to *make* the light come in. Hence, it seems necessary that in order to issue a command, we must take into account the factor whether or not that command is fulfilled by the recipient of the command rather than by some other sources. If a man does not make any effort to bring about a certain state of affairs, then the occurrence of that state of affairs should not be accredited to him. However, we shall not pursue this matter any further as it will certainly lead us too far from our main topics of this discussion.

CHAPTER TWO

META-ETHICS AND SOME
MODIFIED SYSTEMS OF
DEONTIC LOGIC

§ 15. TOWARD A SOUND SYSTEM OF DEONTIC LOGIC

No sooner had the deontic logics gradually taken their shapes than the criticism and misgivings began to multiply in the literature. Most of the mistrust of deontic logic comes from the fact that current systems of deontic logic do not provide us with "sound" systems of the logic of obligation (or permission). That is to say, the systems that we have on hand do not yield semantical interpretations which are intuitively satisfactory as logics which formalize the intuitive notions of obligation, permission, and the like. People want a deontic logician to see to it that his system can be used to formalize or to justify our deontic or normative arguments just as our indicative (or assertoric) logics, such as propositional logic, can be used to formalize and justify our indicative arguments.

In the literature, the criticism of deontic logic has been frequently made in the context of imperative logic. The reason for doing so seems twofold. First, imperative logic has by far a longer history than deontic logic. People are more familiar with, and have a clearer idea of, the much discussed problems and the oft-cited examples in imperative logic than in deontic logic. Indeed, since von Wright constructed his earliest system of deontic logic in the early 1950's, it has not been made immediately clear what the "status" of a deontic sentence is. For instance, is a deontic sentence a report of moral code, or is it used rather to prescribe or to evaluate? Consequently it is not clear whether a deontic sentence is capable of being true or false. On the other hand, it seems unquestionable that an imperative sentence is normally or typically used to issue a command (in the broadest sense), and it seems commonly, if not unanimously, agreed upon that imperative sentences are neither true nor false. [1]

Another reason for treating the problems of deontic logic in imperative logic is this. Many people, notably A. Ross, have taken it to be the case that deontic logic and imperative logic are, to say the least, so closely related to each other that a problem in one logic is automatically or *mutatis mutandis* a problem in the other. This conviction, to be sure, is not groundless. In the next chapter, we want to go even further to say that these two logics are two isomorphic models of the same (normative) logic. Consequently, the problems of imperative logic become the problems of deontic logic, and *vice versa*.

Thus when one wants to argue that the current systems of deontic logic are inadequate, one may take an example from imperative logic to support one's criticism. Indeed, this is what Williams [1963], Keene [1966] and Kenny [1966] have done. A well-known example of a criticism along this line was originally given by A. Ross in connection with imperative logic, [2] but has later been frequently cited in the context of deontic logic.

Ross observed that the following (imperative) argument seemed extremely problematic if not totally invalid:

[1] There are philosophers, notably Leonard, who hold a different view.
[2] See Ross [1941], p. 62 or [1944], p. 38.

(15.1)   Post the letter!

∴ Post the letter or burn it! [3]

However, in our deontic logics, we have shown that

(OT*23) $Op \supset O(p \lor q)$

is a theorem. And, according to propositional logic,

(15.2) $Op \supset . Op \lor Oq$

is a theorem. Now, it seems that either (OT*23) or (15.2) can be used to justify (15.1). But in the opinion of many people, the validity of (15.1) is highly questionable. There-fore, deontic logic, perhaps together with the usual indicative logics, seems to shed no light on, or at least gives no practical guide to, the validity of imperative reasoning. That is, deontic logic is inadequate so far as imperative arguments are concerned. This may be called the problem of the *adequacy of deontic systems*.

We shall not, for the time being, discuss the problems related to arguments like the above one. We leave it until the next chapter when we come to examine the relation between deontic logic and imperative logic.

Another line of attack against present systems of deontic logic is to question whether they can express or formulate certain alleged deontic notions successfully. [4] That is, the (expressive) *completeness of deontic systems*. As we mentioned in section 4, Chisholm has pointed out the fact that certain deontic systems, particularly system vW of von Wright, either cannot formulate the notion of contrary-to-

---

[3] We use '∴' to indicate the alleged conclusion drawn from the lines standing immediately prior to it. The original wording of Ross' example is this: 'Slip the letter into the letter-box!' ∴ 'Slip the letter into the letter-box or burn it!' [*Ibid.*]

[4] See § 4.

duty imperative, or else they contain a contradiction. We have also shown that none of the systems we investigated in Chapter One is immune to this defect. Besides, we also know that we have been so far unable to formulate the concept of commitment in those systems. Now, to this list of formulational or expressive inadequacy, we may add another one: the notion of "conflict of duties". This is a notion closely related, and parallel in many respects, to the notion of contrary-to-duty imperative.

It has often been pointed out that, under certain circumstances, it may be obligatory for us to do a certain act and also obligatory for us not to do it, i.e., to do the negation-act of it. For instance, a certain American youth of today may find himself in the following moral predicament. It is, on the one hand, obligatory for him to answer the summons of his country to go to fight in Vietnam. But, on the other hand, it is also obligatory for him to listen to his conscience and not to go to fight there. Obviously, this situation cannot be adequately expressed in our deontic systems in the last chapter without generating a contradiction, because in each of those systems, it can be shown that

(15.3)   It is not the case that a certain act and its negation are both obligatory.

In short, the following, or its variant, is a theorem of those systems:

(OT*19) $\sim (Op \mathbin{\&} O \sim p)$

Therefore, we have another dilemma very similar to Chisholm's. Namely, either we are unable to express the notion of conflicting duties in our systems of deontic logic, or else they contain a contradiction.

The classic solution to the problem of conflicting duties,

or the common explanation of this problem, is to appeal to the well-known distinction, first made by William David Ross, between so-called *prima-facie* duties and actual ones. Many people today are still fond of following Ross in saying that for the American young man, for instance, it is his *prima-facie* duty to go to fight in Vietnam, and it is also his *prima-facie* duty not to go to fight there. However, he will, under the particular circumstance in question, find out or "see" which course of action he *really* ought to take, namely, to arrive at his *actual* duty in that particular situation.

This solution, although attractive and convenient at first sight, seems on second glance less than satisfactory. The very idea of drawing a distinction between *prima-facie* duties and actual duties in the case of conflicting obligations lies on a rather strong presupposition—that whenever two sets of moral rules are incompatible, there is a meta-rule (explicitly or otherwise) which directs that one of these sets overrules the other, or that both sets are overruled by a third set of rules—which is problematic and questionable. That this is indeed the case will be seen in the latter sections along with our discussion of the formal theory of ethics and our presentation of an alternative approach to the problem.[5]

The alternative we shall adopt, and thus one of the main purposes of this chapter, is to develop an alternative semantic theory of deontic logic in which both Chisholm's dilemma and the dilemma of conflicting obligations, and

5 See especially § 17.

hopefully, even the paradox of the Good Samaritan can be satisfactorily accounted for.

§16. DEONTIC VARIABLES RANGE OVER CM-ACT-PROPOSITIONS

The first step toward a semantic interpretation of deontic logic is to spell out the range of the deontic variables. We have, on two previous occasions, familiarized ourselves with two different readings of deontic variables. In von Wright's system vW and Fisher and Åqvist's system FÅ, we let a deontic variable range over act-types. In these systems, it is an act-type that is said to be obligatory, permissible or what not. Later, we indicated that deontic logicians nowadays have much favored another practice, namely, to let a deontic variable take not act-types but propositions or states of affairs as its values. According to them, it is a proposition or a state of affairs that is said to be obligatory, permissible, and so on. Neither of these two readings of deontic variables proved to be totally satisfactory.

First of all, it should be kept in mind that what is performed by any person at any time in any place is an act-instance, namely, an instance of an act-type, rather than an act-type. It would be a category mistake if we should allow ourselves to talk about the performance of act-types. No one can by any means perform an act-type which is an abstract entity, or as von Wright calls it, a set of "act qualifying properties". To say that a certain act-type, e.g., smoking, is permissible is perhaps only an abbreviated way of saying that every act-instance which falls into the category of smoking, i.e., the individual act of smoking, is permissible. Or, any individual act which has the character-istic properties of smoking is permissible. It is clear that what we need in this connection are three different types of symbols rather than just deontic variables in order to successfully symbolize sentences like

(16.1)   Smoking is permissible.

To be specific, we need variables for individual acts, variables for act-types and finally a symbol for a predicate which means that "① falls into the category of ②" or "① has the characteristic properties of ②", or the like. [1] But this symbolism seems only to point to another problem: quantifiers become indispensable in deontic logic. [2] Or, in other words, no satisfactory deontic logic is possible other than a quantified theory if we want deontic logic to be a logic of obligation which formalizes our intuitive deontic notions. For (16.1) will then mean

(16.2)   For every act-instance, if it falls into the cate-gory of smoking, then it is permissible.

It may be pointed out, however, that more often than not we do find moral codes expressed in such an unspecified manner as exemplified by the following examples:

(16.3)   Thou shalt not kill.   (Ten Commandments)

(16.4)   Do not do to others what you do not want others to do to you.   (Confucius)

(16.5)   An unexamined life is not worth living. (Socrates)

---

1 The circled numeral notation is borrowed from Quine. See Quine [1950], p. 131.

2 Hintikka is the first philosopher who pointed out the indispen-sability of quantifiers in deontic logics similar to system vW. See Hintikka [1957].

(16.6)   Be prepared.   (A motto for Boy Scouts)
and
(16.7)   Honesty is the best policy.   (English saying)

These examples show that moral codes are usually expressed in an obscure manner. They resemble (16.1) more than (16.2). In particular, they do not mention, or even explicitly presuppose the existence of, the individual acts to which these codes may apply. However, attention must also be called to the fact that a moral code would fail to direct people's action should there be no "bridge rules" to connect particular act-instances to a certain moral code.

Another difficulty in the usual conception of a deontic variable has already been pointed out earlier in section 2. It is a problem associated with the notion of act and the notion of performance. Does the notion of an act, as we asked before, entail or presuppose the notion of performance? The answer seems to be this. If we take 'act' to mean act-instances, then the answer is "yes". But if by 'act' we mean act-types, then the answer is quite uncertain. We may even incline to say that the answer is in the negative. Or, at least we have in this case come up with a different notion of performance. Consider the following example. If we say that an act-type, e.g., smoking, is performed, this seems at most a disguised way of saying that an act-instance, i.e., a smoking-instance or an individual smoking, which falls into a certain category, i.e., smoking, is performed. Since there exists such a discrepancy between these two concepts of act, a deontic logician must decide which one of these two notions of act, or both of them, he wants to incorporate into his system. Otherwise, he will find himself talking about act-qualifying properties and the actualization of certain act-instances which have these properties indiscriminately. Lack of such discrimination is responsible for the awkward situation in system vW where we found ourselves saying that if the performance of an act (-type) is so and so, then......is such and such. But no one can ever perform an act-type! The difficulty is avoided, of course, if we let a deontic variable range over individual acts, and construct deontic logic as a quantified theory.

A similar difficulty may appear when we have not carefully enough specified what we mean when we say that a deontic variable ranges over propositions. For instance, we found ourselves reading 'Op ⊃ Pp' as "What is obligatory is permissible" or "If something is obligatory, then it is permissible". However, these latter expressions seem rather to be legitimate renderings of '(p)(Op ⊃ Pp)'. But this difficulty seems negligible, because, as in other well-established branches of logic, for instance, propositional logic, when we assert an open sentence, we have a convention that the sentence holds for all values of its (free) variables.

One of the advantages of taking propositions as the range of deontic variables lies, however, in the fact that this practice makes deontic logic more akin to other branches of logic, so that what is already known in other branches of logic will automatically shed light on the development of deontic logic. We saw this in the last chapter when we constructed certain deontic logics as subsystems of the corresponding alethic modal logics. But, insofar as we want to talk about our actions in deontic logic, the notion of an act of a certain type must be at least implicitly, if not otherwise, contained in the notion of the propositions we have in mind as the range of the deontic variables. Indeed

this is clearly so as can be seen in the way we managed
to interpret a deontic sentence OT*—OS5*. As we recall,
a formula like

Op

where 'p' stands for a proposition, was understood as saying
that to bring it about that p is obligatory. The notion of
bringing-it-about-that certainly entails endeavorings, or in
short, acts.

In what follows, we shall also take propositions as
values of a deontic variable. But we shall do so in a more
specific manner. We shall not only maintain that it is the
class of act-instances that concerns us in deontic logic, but
also agree that when, where, and by whom an act is performed must be specified. In other words, we shall have in
our newly devised and interpreted systems of deontic logic
sentences of the following form:

(16.8)   It is obligatory that ① at the time ② in the
             place ③ brings it about that ④

That is,

(16.9)   It is obligatory that someone at a certain time
             in a certain place brings about a certain act.

Here, the '④' in (16.8) stands for an act-type. For instance,
we may say that

(16.10)   It is obligatory that John on July 10, 1968, in Room
             14, Morrill Hall, brings it about that cleaning
             and putting in order.

Here cleaning and putting in order is an act-type. It goes
without saying that (16.10) means the same as

(16.11)   John ought to clean and put in order Room 14
             of Morrill Hall on July 10, 1968.

only that in (16.10) we have a sentence of the following

form:
(16.12)   John...brings it about that cleaning and putting in order.

while in (16.11) we have a sentence of the following form:
(16.13)   John...cleans and puts in order..... .

We shall call sentences like (16.12) or (16.13) which designate someone's doing something *act-sentences*, and call the propositions they stand for *act-propositions*. In particular, we shall say that an act-sentence like (16.12) is an act-sentence in *explicit form* if it exhibits the following grammatical form

(16.14) x brings it about that p.

where 'x' stands for a certain agent or actor, and 'p' for a certain act-type. When there is no danger of confusion, we shall use either form of an act-sentence. But when we need to be precise, an act sentence in explicit form is called for.

An act-sentence may be put in a more specific manner by adding several types of modification. In particular, we might, as we suggested above, manifestly express when and where the bringing-about depicted by an act-sentence takes place. That is, we may write an act-sentence in the following form

(16.15) x at time t in place w brings it about that p.

In (16.15) we specified at what time and in what place the bringing about endeavored by x takes place. The two modifications, namely spatial and temporal ones, say, in short, under what circumstances x brings it about that p. Thus, we shall say that when time and location are specified, an act-sentence is *circumstantialized*. Circumstantialized act-sentences will be called CM-*act-sentences*.

They are standard sentences we shall encounter in the latter discussion.

A special remark may be in order. Earlier we criticized the use of act-types as the values of a deontic variable. But now we employ act-types again. However, it should be clear that act-types are now used in a rather special way. We, so to speak, circumstantialize an act-type and hence individualize it. Thus what we have obtained are individual acts rather than act-types.

Let us say that a CM-act-sentence stands for a CM-act-proposition, and let us declare that deontic variables range over CM-act-propositions. Or, as some logicians may want to say, that deontic variables take CM-act-sentences as their substituents.

For the sake of brevity we shall symbolize (6.15) as

(16. 16) $(x, t, w)\,\mathrm{p}$

where '(x, t, w)' may be called the CM-*parameters* of (16.16). It is often convenient to hold the CM-parameters constant, hence we introduce the following abbreviation:

(C 16.1)   When the CM-parameters '(x, t, w)' is constant in a formula or in a discourse, we shall omit the parameter and write a starred sentence. [3]

An act is not done if and only if its negation-act is done. Hence we have the following "equivalence":

(16.17) $\ulcorner \sim (x,\ t,\ w)\,\mathrm{A} \urcorner \equiv \ulcorner (x,\ t,\ w) \sim \mathrm{A} \urcorner$

It follows that although expressions like

(16.18) $\sim \mathrm{p}^{*}$

are ambiguous, the ambiguity is indeed harmless. Likewise,

---

[3] Cf. (16. 18) below. For an effective way of making this abbreviation, see section 19.

(16.19) $\ulcorner (x,\ t,\ w)\,A\ \&\ (x,\ t,\ w)\,B \urcorner$

has the same truth condition as

(16.20) $\ulcorner (x,\ t,\ w)\,(A\ \&\ B) \urcorner$

Hence, the following equivalence holds:

(16.21) $\ulcorner (x,\ t,\ w)\,A\ \&\,(x,\ t,\ w)\,B \urcorner \equiv \ulcorner (x,\ t,\ w,)$
            $(A\ \&\ B) \urcorner$

Other sentential connectives are defined in the usual way. Again we realize that connectives like '$\sim$', '$\&$', 'v',...are used in two different ways. But this ambiguity is trivial and innocuous.

§ 17. THE INTERPRETATION OF 'O' IN TERMS OF MORAL RULES

The second step toward a sound system of deontic logic is to find a suitable meaning or interpretation for the deontic operator 'O' (or 'P' as the case may be). This task is generally neglected by deontic logicians. As we saw in the last chapter, all the systems we examined take either 'O' or 'P' as a deontic operator standing for a certain pimitive deontic notion. Although these primitive deontic operators have been intuitively rendered as "obligatory" for 'O' or "permissible" for 'P', these notions have never been precisely defined. It happens that to leave these primitive notions vaguely or ambiguously understood accounts indeed for part of the reason why the resulting deontic systems are so unsatisfactory and why the previously mentioned dilemmas seem always to plague those systems.

The main purpose of this section is thus to assign a precise meaning to, or make an exact interpretation of, the deontic operator 'O'. We shall no longer tacitly understand 'O' as standing for a roughly conceived notion of obligation. We shall explain obligation in terms of other concepts. The need to make the meaning of 'O' clear and precise can be easily appreciated. Simply try to answer the following questions: How is it that we are obliged to do so and so? What obliges us to do such and such? What makes it the case that thus and thus is obligatory?

It is easy to see that different authorities may oblige

us to perform different acts under different circumstances. So that acts are obligatory or not for different reasons under different conditions. In short, the notion of obligation is not an absolute notion. An act is obligatory or not relative to a certain authority which obliges, or fails to oblige, us to perform that act. Different authorities may issue different types of obligation. That is to say, when there are different authorities which oblige us to do this or that, we have different notions of obligation: obligation[1], obligation[2], obligation[3], and so on. 'Obligation' is a blanket term, there are a great many different notions under this name.

We shall say that it is a set of moral rules which obliges us to do so and so. Or, in our terminology, we shall say that $\ulcorner (x, t, w)A \urcorner$ or A^* is obligatory if and only if a set of rules R *requires* that A be brought about by x at t in w. Different sets of rules may direct us differently, that is, issue to us different obligations. Let us, hence, relativize an obligation O_R as that which is directed or required by rules R. In short, we will put down the following definition:

(D17.1) $\ulcorner O_R A^* \urcorner =_{Df}$ R requires that A^*

So defined, the notion of obligation is no longer an absolute notion. (It becomes relative to a set of rules.)

Other deontic notions can be likewise defined. For instance, $\ulcorner P_R A^* \urcorner$ is the case if and only if R does not require that $\ulcorner \sim A^* \urcorner$, i.e., if and only if R *allows* that A^*. And $\ulcorner F_R A^* \urcorner$ is the case if and only if R requires that $\ulcorner \sim A^* \urcorner$, or, if and only if R *prohibits* that A^*. Finally, $\ulcorner I_R A^* \urcorner$ is the case if and only if R does not require that A^* nor does it require that $\ulcorner \sim A^* \urcorner$. That is to say, R allows that A* and also allows that $\ulcorner\sim\! A^*\urcorner$. That is,

(D17.2) $\ulcorner P_R A^*\urcorner =_{Df} \ulcorner\sim\! O_R\sim\! A^*\urcorner$

(D17.3) $\ulcorner F_R A^*\urcorner =_{Df} \ulcorner\sim\! P_R A^*\urcorner$

(D17.4) $\ulcorner I_R A^* =_{Df} \ulcorner P_R A^* \,\&\, P_R\sim\! A^*\urcorner$

Henceforth, when we talk about obligation, we always mean an *indexed* one, i e., either obligation[1], or obligation[2], or obligation[3], and so on, which are, respectively, derived from, or backed up by, moral rules R_1, R_2, R_3, and so forth.

We shall say that a CM-act-proposition p* is *determinate* under a set of (moral) rules R, if R requires that p*, or it prohibits that p*, or it allows that p* and also allows that $\sim\! p^*$. That is to say, p* is determinate under R if and only if the following (17.1) holds:

(17.1) $O_R p^* \text{ v } F_R p^* \text{ v } I_R p^*$

We shall also say that a set of rules is used to *determine* the "deontic value" of a CM-act-proposition. A set of rules R_i determines that p* is obligatory[i] if the set of rules requires that p*. It determines that p* is permissible[i] if the set of rules allows that p*, and so on. Let us call "obligatoriness[i]", "forbiddenness[i]" and "indifference" deontic values of a CM-act-proposition under R_i and denote them by '0', '2' and '1', respectively. Thus, when R_i determines that p* is obligatory[i], we shall write '$R_i(p^*)=0$', and when R_i determines that p* is indifferent[i], we write '$R_i(p^*) =1$', and so on. Hence, (17.1) may also be written as

(17.2) $R_i(p^*) =0 \text{ v } R_i(p^*) =2 \text{ v } R_i(p^*) =1$

The notion of determinateness under a set of rules can also be extended to a class of CM-act-propositions. Let us say that a set Δ of CM-act-propositions is *determinate* under R_i if every member of Δ is determinate under R_i. And we shall use 'Δ_i' to denote the set of all CM-act-proposition determinate under the set of rules R_i. It turns out that, for each i, Δ_i is the set of all CM-act-propositions.

A set of rules R_i is said to be *consistent* if and only if there is no CM-act-proposition p* such that (17.3) below holds:

(17.3) $O_R p^*$ & $O_R \sim p^*$

otherwise, R_i is inconsistent. In other words, a set of rules is said to be consistent if it does not require that a certain proposition and its negation both be brought about by someone at a certain time in a certain place. Otherwise, the set of rules is said to be inconsistent.

Two sets of rules, R_i and R_j, are said to be *compatible* if and only if $R_i \cup R_j$ is consistent. Otherwise, they are *incompatible*.

Let us, from now on, talk only about consistent sets of rules. We shall say that a set R_i of rules *overrules* another set R_j *with respect to,* or under, a set of meta-rules Q if and only if Q directs that the determination of R_i has precedence over that of R_j. Roughly speaking, a set of rules overrules another set under a set of meta-rules if the meta-rules dictate that the first set of rules takes the place of the second in making moral judgment or evaluation. And we shall say that R_i *properly* overrules R_j if R_i overrules R_j and $R_i \neq R_j$.

If we let 'Over' stand for the overruling relation, and read 'Over (R_1, R_2, Q)' as "R_1 overrules R_2 under Q", then it is easy to see that the following (17.4) holds:

(17.4)   Over (R_1, R_2, Q) & Over (R_2, R_3, Q). $\supset$ Over (R_1, R_3, Q)

We shall say that the overruling relation is *quasi*-transitive in the sense of (17.4). It is also *quasi*-nonsymmetric defined similarly, as can be easily seen.

A set $\sum$ of sets of rules is said to be *closed under* (meta-rules) Q if and only if there is a member R_i of $\sum$ such that R_i properly overrules every other member of $\sum$ under Q. Otherwise, $\sum$ is *open under* Q. Further, a set $\sum$ of sets of rules is said to be *hierarchical under* Q if some member of $\sum$ is properly overruled by some other member of $\sum$. Otherwise, $\sum$ is *insular under* Q. To be more precise, we shall say that a set $\sum$ of sets of rules is *hierarchical under* Q *at the point* $R_j (R_j \in \sum)$ if and only if there is a $R_i \in \sum$ such that $R_i \neq R_j$ and Over (R_i, R_j, Q). Hence, a hierarchical set (of sets of rules) under Q is a set of sets (of rules) which is hierarchical under Q at some points. And an insular set under Q is a set of sets which is hierarchical under Q at no point.

Just as the concept of hierarchy under Q may be further relativized, the concept of openness of a set of sets under Q can also be so specified. We shall say that a set $\sum$ of more than one set is *open under* Q *at the point* R_j, if and only if there is no $R_i \in \sum$ such that $R_i \neq R_j$ and Over (R_i, R_j, Q). Hence, a set of (more than one) set(s) is open under Q if it is open at some points. Of course, the concept of closure of a set of sets may also be likewise relativized. And a set of sets is closed under Q if it is closed under Q at every point except one which stands for the set that overrules every other set.

We may draw a chart to illustrate the (proper) overruling relation under Q between sets of rules. Let circles denote sets of rules. A blank circle 'o' means that the set is not overruled (under Q) and a darkened circle '●' means that the set is overruled. And let denote the overruling relation under Q where the set **re-**presented by a circle (must be a darkened one) standing at the point of the arrow is overruled under Q by the set represented by a circle (may be a blank one) standing at the tail of the arrow. Now, the following chart 1 shows that the illustrated set of rules is open

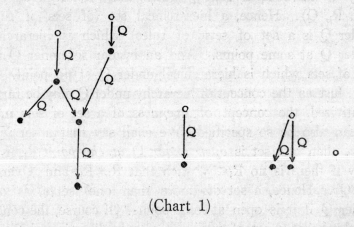

(Chart 1)

because it is open at more than one point. The following chart 2, however, illustrates a set of sets which is closed. It is open at exactly one point representing the set that overrules every other set.

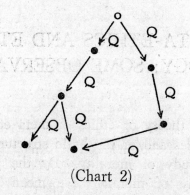

(Chart 2)

Finally, let us define the consistency of a set of sets of rules. A set $\sum = \{R_1, R_2, R_3,...\}$ of sets of rules is said to be *absolutely consistent* if and only if

$$\bigcup_{i=1, 2, 3, \cdots} R_i$$

is consistent (in the sense defined above). Otherwise, $\sum$ is absolutely inconsistent. And $\sum$ is said to be *practically consistent under* Q if and only if

$$\bigcup_{j=1, 2, 3, \cdots} R_k{}^j$$

is nonempty and consistent, where each $R_k{}^j$ is a point at which $\sum$ is open under Q. Otherwise, $\sum$ is practically inconsistent under Q. Absolute consistency entails practical consistency.

§ 18. META-ETHICS AND ETHICO-SOCIOLOGY: SOME OBSERVATIONS

In a formal theory of ethics or meta-ethics, we study the basic principles and/or the basic structure of an ethical theory or the study of morality. By the phrase 'ethical theory' or 'study of morality' we mean the results of reflecting on and idealization of the moral phenomena we have been experiencing. To theorize is to construct and reconstruct. And in the process of construction and reconstruction, a certain degree of idealization is always unavoidable. Hence, it is no wonder that certain features in our reconstruction of morality do not completely mirror their counterparts in the actual morality which we vaguely experience in our daily life. For instance, a certain distinction may be very hard to draw in actual morality, because the difference is so slight and delicate as to easily escape our attention. But for the sake of our discussion we might find it necessary to emphasize the distinction and bring it into the focus of our attention. Therefore, we do not claim that what we shall have said below is a faithful description of our morality; we only intend that our theory serves as a "model" which bears the basic and important features, perhaps in a somewhat artificial manner, of our morality.

Another remark is also called for. We are not going to construct a complete theory of meta-ethics. What we shall try to do is to develop the theory to such an extent that is sufficient for explaining or solving the deontic problems we set forth for ourselves.

We shall develop the theory of meta-ethics in a set of "assumptions" and "consequences" making free use of the concepts and notations we established in the last section. First, a list of assumptions. Each of them will be followed by some explanation or intuitive rendering.

(Assumption 18.1) *An ethical system of moralities* ⟨S, Q⟩ *is an ordered pair consisting of a set* S *of sets of moral rules and a set* Q *of meta-rules.* (We shall call S a morality).

Basically we think of a morality as what can be summarized in a set of moral rules. Hence we identify a set of moral rules with a morality. In an actual situation, however, this is not so clear. Although we may, for instance, think of the Ten Commandments as forming a set of moral rules, i.e., a morality, which many people take as their guiding principles of life, in most other cases we do not have a set of moral rules so explicitly spelt out. For instance, we might ask what is the set of rules constituting the morality to which American college students of today submit themselves. The answer is quite unclear. We may even doubt whether there exists such a set of moral rules or rule-like things.

In general, a morality is only very vaguely "circumscribed" by a certain moral ideal which is more or less shared by people in a certain community. What one ought to do under certain circumstances is often left open and remains to be interpreted by established moral authority in that community. Nevertheless, we shall assume here that a set of rules can always be, at least in principle, written down.

We also take it to be the case that there are different

moralities in the world or in our society. Each of them is depicted by a set of moral rules. Hence, we have a set of sets of moral rules. (We do not claim that this system is a finite set or an infinite set. We leave this question open.) But a set of sets of moral rules is not by itself a system of morality or an ethical system. To have a system of morality, we need also a set of meta-rules which directs, for example, whether one set of moral rules overrules another when the two are in conflict. Again, it must be pointed out that we do not experience such a clear-cut distinction between moral rules and meta-rules in our daily life.

(Assumption 18. 2) *Every morality is consistent.*

That is to say, no set of moral rules will oblige us to do something and at the same time do its negation. In the symbolism we developed in the last section, this can be put down as follows: For every set R_i of moral rules and for every CM-act-proposition p^*, it is not the case that $R_i(p^*) = 0$ and $R_i(\sim p^*) = 0$. To assume this consistency property of a set of moral rules is indispensable. For, otherwise, we will be unable to act morally *and* consistently. An inconsistent set of moral rules, for instance, may oblige one to go and not to go fight in Vietnam.

(Assumption 18.3) *In a system $\langle S, Q \rangle$ of moralities, some moralities properly overrule others under Q.*

That is to say, there are occasions when CM-act-propositions are put under the determination of different mutually incompatible sets of moral rules, and some of them give way to others.

(Assumption 18.4) *The set of all CM-act-propositions determinate under every set of moral rules is the universal set* V *of CM-act-propositions.*

In other words, every CM-act-proposition is subject to moral judgment and becomes determinate under every set of moral rules. Or, as we may also say, any of our acts is submitted to morality.

This assumption can be derived from our definition of the set of all CM-propositions determinate under a set of rule. But for the sake of emphasis we list it here.

From the above assumptions, we may draw the following consequences:

(Consequence 18.1) *There are at least two sets of moral rules in a system of moralities.*

Pf. By (Assumption 18. 3)

(Consequence 18.2) *There are at least two incompatible sets of moral rules in a system of moralities.*

Pf. Similar: (Consequence 18.1)

(Consequence 18.3) *A system of moralities is hierarchical.*

Pf. Similar: (Consequence 18.1)

(Consequence 18.4) *A system of moralities is absolutely inconsistent.*

Pf. As a corollary of (Consequence 18.2)

This theorem which sounds surprising at first glance does, nevertheless, reflect our moral phenomena very well. We do experience the fact that we have submitted ourselves to different moralities which are not compatible with one another. The morality of being a good parent, for example, may not be compatible with the morality of being a good husband. The morality of the battle field in Vietnam may be at great variance with the morality of a university campus. And the morality for the man in the street may be quite different from the morality for the justices of the Supreme Court, and so on. Indeed, occasions may often arise when we find ourselves directed by two sets of incompatible rules simultaneously, and no meta-rules dictate which of these sets of rules overrules the other, or dictate that they are both overruled by still another set of rules. Hence, it seems that what this theorem says is nothing other than a simple truth in our morality. This fact should be recognized in order to prevent certain false convictions about our morality.

It seems that we should not make an unreflecting use of Ross' distinction between actual duties and *prima-facie* ones to solve every case of conflicting obligations. Although the distinction may be drawn theoretically, it is naive to think that we can apply this distinction to solve every problem of conflicting obligations. For this conviction presupposes that when there are incompatible sets of rules which generate conflicting duties there is a meta-rule (explicit or otherwise) which directs that one of these sets overrules the other, or that a third set of rules overrules these two sets, and, besides, that this set of overruling rules will finally give us the answer what is our actual duty. This, however, is too strong a presupposition as we suggested in § 15. Hence, the above-mentioned conviction seems far too oversimplified a solution to the problem of conflicting duties. It leaves us with a false idealistic view of morality that, under given circumstances, there is always a set of rules which will tell us what we *really* should do under those circumstances. Had this been the case, our moral life would be much easier to lead; and many more people would go to bed every night happier and with a much more peaceful mind. Unfortunately, the truth is that our moral system is inconsistent absolutely or practically and so we may find ourselves simultaneously submitted to some incompatible sets of moral rules. All the tragedies and tears are not always superficial. There are the genuine moral dilemmas, moral predicaments or moral perplexities! They are insolvable by any means, not to mention the verbal distinction between actual and *prima-facie* duties, so far as our system of moralities remains inconsistent and so far as we try to solve the problem not by cutting the Gordian knot but by carefully untying it.

However, to include (Consequence 18.4) in our theory is by no means to claim that a system of moralities *must* be inconsistent. What we claim is only that our system of moralities *is* inconsistent. There is no reason why there should not be, and indeed it is welcome that there is, a consistent system of moralities in our world. (And, hence, our (Consequence 18. 4) becomes false of such a system.) Many national and international problems come from the fact that we tolerate or are prepared to tolerate inconsistent systems of moralities. A consistent system of moralities may well emerge in the remote future. But this question is beyond our concern here.

The above assumptions and consequences may be thought of as some observations in meta-ethics.

Some additional remarks. Although we proved that a system of moralities is absolutely inconsistent, we are unable either to prove or to disprove that it is practically consistent. That is a question we leave open. We also leave it open whether or not a system of moralities is infinitely hierarchical.

Ethico-sociology studies the organization and structure of morality in a society. It stresses the relation between man as member of society and morality as a social institution. The following are some observations, again, arranged as assumptions and consequences.

(Assumption 18.5) *A society institutionalizes various roles for its members to play.*

For example, a man and a woman become husband and wife because of the social institution of marriage. One person is a teacher of another owing to the social institution of schooling. A man becomes the commander-in-chief of his fellow men because there is a social institution of a nation. And a man becomes a priest due to the fact that there is a certain religious body, and so on. All the political, religious, economic, and educational organizations, and so on, are social institutions in the wider sense. Even the natural relation between mother and child is institutionalized in a civilized society like ours. Motherhood becomes a socially institutionalized role which a woman plays in a society. It is a role quite different from, for example, that which a mother duck plays to her ducklings along the banks of the Red Cedar River.

(Assumption 18.6)   *At any time, every man plays at least one role.*

(Assumption 18.7)   *Some men play different roles simultaneously.*

For instance, one may at the same time be a husband and a father, a mathematician, a soldier, and a philosopher, and so on.

(Assumption 18.8)   *A society institutionalizes with each role exactly one morality.*

(We shall call this morality the morality associated with this role.)

(Assumption 18.9) *Different roles have different moralities.*

(Assumption 18.10) *If a man plays a role, then the society which he is in puts him under, or submits him to, the morality associated with that role.* (We shall also say that a man *submits himself to* the morality.)

Let us now define the notion of one morality overruling another as meaning that the set of rules of the first morality overrules the set of rules of the second morality. Here we let a certain set Q of meta-rules tacitly understood.

(Assumption 18.11) *If a man submits himself to incompatible moralities, and there is another morality which overrules these moralities, then the man submits himself to the overruling morality.*

If there are many overruling moralities, mutually compatible or not, then he submits himself to all of them.

From these assumptions the following consequences can be inferred.

(Consequence 18.5) *A society institutionalizes a system of moralities.*

Pf. From (Assumption 18.5) and (Assumption 18.8)

(Consequence 18.6) *Every man (in a society) submits himself to at least one morality at a time.*

Pf. From (Assumption 18.6), (Assumption 18.8), and (Assumption 18.10).

(Consequence 18.7) *There are at least two different moralities in a society.*

Pf. From (Assumption 18.7), (Assumption 18.8), (Assumption 18.9), and (Assumption 18.10)

(Consequence 18.8) *Some men submit themselves to different moralities simultaneously.*

Pf. Similar: (Consequence 18.7)

It may be mentioned that from the results we stated above, we can neither prove nor disprove the following thesis:

(18.1)   Some men do submit themselves to incompatible moralities simultaneously.

Hence, we leave open the following "corollary" of (18.1)

(18.2)   The conflict of obligation is possible.

A man may find that he ought to do something and at the same time ought not to do it. Or, he may find that he ought to perform a certain act and at the same time ought to perform its negation. A moral predicament. [1]

A final remark may be in order before we come to the end of this section. It should also be realized that in our theory we can neither prove nor disprove the following:

(18.3)   For any two incompatible moralities, it is always the case that one of them overrules the other.

or

(18.4)   For any two incompatible moralities, there is always another morality which overrules them.

Should (18.3) or (18.4) be true in a society, then we could prove that the system of morality in that society is practically consistent povided that the system is finitely hierarchical. However, as we mentioned in the last section, the practical consistency of a system of morality is left

---

1 The truth of this statement should be determined in a meta-theory of morality rather than in a system of morality.

open. This should be so, because of the undecidability of (18.3) and (18.4).

§ 19. THREE SYSTEMS OF DEONTIC LOGIC: CMO$_R$T*, CMO$_R$S4* AND CMO$_R$S5*

In accordance with what we have developed in §§ 15-16, we shall outline here three new systems CMO$_R$T*, CMO$_R$S4* and CMO$_R$S5* of deontic logic which are, respectively, variant systems of OT*, OS4* and OS5* of the last chapter.

First, the vocabulary (common to all three systems):

(I) Vocabulary
  i) Variables for agents or actors: 'x_1', 'x_2', 'x_3',...
  ii) Variables for time: 't_1', 't_2', 't_3',...
  iii) Variables for location: 'w_1', 'w_2', 'w_3',...
  iv) Act (-type) variables: 'p', 'q', 'r', 'p_1',...
  v) Deontic connectives: '~', '&', 'v', '⊃', '≡'
  vi) Sentential connectives: '~', '&', 'v', '⊃', '≡'
  viii) Parameter delimiters: '(',')'
  ix) Grouping indicators: '[',']'

Next come the formation rules. They are again common to all three systems.

(II) Formation rules
  i) An act (-type) variable standing alone is a *deontic term*.
  ii) If θ_1 and θ_2 are deontic terms, so are $\ulcorner \sim \theta_1 \urcorner$, $\ulcorner [\theta_1 \& \theta_2] \urcorner$, $\ulcorner [\theta_1 \vee \theta_2] \urcorner$, $\ulcorner [\theta_1 \supset \theta_2] \urcorner$ and $\ulcorner [\theta_1 \equiv \theta_2] \urcorner$.
  iii) If α, β, γ are, respectively, variables for agent, time and location and ϕ is a deontic term, then $\ulcorner (\alpha, \beta, \gamma)\phi \urcorner$ is a CM-*act-sentence* (form).

iv) If X and Y are CM-act-sentences, so are $\ulcorner\sim X\urcorner$, $\ulcorner[X \mathbin{\&} Y]\urcorner$, $\ulcorner[X \vee Y]\urcorner$, $\ulcorner[X \supset Y]\urcorner$, and $\ulcorner[X \equiv Y]\urcorner$.

v) A CM-act-sentence is a *wff* (well-formed formula).

vi) If A is a wffs, so is $\ulcorner O_R A\urcorner$.

vii) If A and B are wffs, so are $\ulcorner\sim A\urcorner$, $\ulcorner[A \mathbin{\&} B]\urcorner$, $\ulcorner[A \vee B]\urcorner$, $\ulcorner[A \supset B]\urcorner$ and $\ulcorner[A \equiv B]\urcorner$.

viii) An expression is a deontic term only if it is so formed by i)-ii); it is a CM-act-sentence only if it is so formed by iii)-iv); and it is a wff only if it is so formed by v)-vii).

A remark is called for. We have declared above that a deontic operator like 'O_R' takes CM-act-sentences as its operands. According to this proclamation, it seems that certain deontic expressions such as

(19.1) $\qquad O_R O_R (x,\ t,\ w)\,\mathrm{p}$

in which iterated deontic operators occur, are not well-formed, because

(19.2) $\qquad O_R (x,\ t,\ w)\,\mathrm{p}$

which is the operand of the first occurrence of 'O_R' in (19.1) is *not* a CM-act-sentence, although

(19.3) $\qquad (x,\ t,\ w)\,\mathrm{p}$

which is a sub-sentence of (19.2) but is *not* the operand of the first occurrence of 'O_R' in (19.1), is. Let us say that the first occurrence of 'O_R' in (19.1) has (19.2) as its scope, and it refers, indirectly perhaps, to (19.3). Let us use the following chart to convey the general idea of this (indirect) reference.

(19.4)

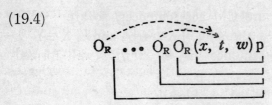

where the broken arrows indicate reference, the "cornered" lines indicate, respectively, the scopes of the operators standing immediately left of them. It may be noted that we may have tildes in addition to deontic operators among the operators we mentioned above. We shall call any occurrence of a deontic operator except the right-most one in an iterated series of deontic operators an iterated operator. For example, all the occurrences of 'O_R' in (19.4) except the last one are iterated. In addition, we shall count the iterated deontic operators from right to left as first-degree iterated deontic operator, second-degree deontic operator, third-degree deontic operator, and so on, while an uniterated deontic operator may be thought of as a zero-degree iterated operator. For example, the first (left-most) occurrence of 'O_R' in (19.5) below is a fourth-degree iterated deontic operator in that expression, and the last (right-most) occurrence of 'O_R' in the same expression is a zero-degree iterated operator.

(19.5) $\sim O_R O_R O_R \sim O_R O_R (x,\ t,\ w)\, p$

Now, our proclamation about the operands of a deontic operator may be restated as follows: an uniterated or isolated deontic operator, as we said before, takes as its operand CM-act-propositions; a first-degree iterated deontic operator takes as its operand a deontic expression in which there is an uniterated deontic operator operating over an CM-act-proposition which the first-degree iterated deontic operator indirectly refers to. Likewise, we can specify the operands of a deontic operator of a higher degree. In fact, a set of recursive definitions can be given to specify more precisely the operand of any deontic operator of any degree. However, we shall not do it here, because the main interest of setting up those definitions is to characterize the set of well-formed formulas in our new system(s) of deontic logic. This job is done effectively by the formation rules we put down above.

Deontic operators other than 'O_R', namely, 'P_R', 'F_R' and 'I_R' are defined in the usual way.

Before we can see in what sense we shall make our present systems of deontic logic CMO_RT^*—CMO_RS5^*, respectively, variant systems of OT^*—$OS5^*$, we shall first set up a set of rules which can be used to effectively enumerate CM-act-sentences of the following form:

(19.5) $(x_i, t_j, w_m)\,p$

where p is a deontic variable.

We have on several earlier occasions used expressions like

$$(x, t, w)\,p$$

in which CM-parameters are not subscripted. This should be regarded as only an informal way of writing down a CM-act-sentence. Indeed we listed at the beginning of this section as variables for these parameters only ones with subscripts. The reason for doing so should become obvious in a few moments when we have set down the rules for enumerating the above-mentioned CM-act-sentences.

Now, the rules:

i) Let Φ be a function which maps the set of CM-act-sentences $\{B | B = (x_i, t_j, w_m) A\}$ to the set of superscripted starred sentences $\{A^{*^k} | k$ is a natural number} in the following manner:

$$\Phi(B) = A^{* (z_1^i \bullet z_2^j \bullet z_3^m)} \qquad \text{i.e., } k = z_1^i \bullet z_2^j \bullet z_3^m$$

where 'z_s' denotes the sth prime in the natural order, namely, 2, 3, 5, ... For example, $\Phi((x_1, t_1, w_1) p) = p^{*^{2^1 \bullet 3^1 \bullet 5^1}} = p^{*^{30}}$. Due to the unique factorization theorem, this enumeration is unique and unambiguous. We shall call k the *index* of the starred sentence p^*.

ii) Take p^*'s, arrange them according to the magnitude of their indices. We then have an enumeration

$$p^{*1} \ p^{*2} \ p^{*3}, \ ...$$

iii) Do the same as prescribed in ii) to q^*'s, r^*'s, p_1^*'s, q_1^*'s, r_1^*'s, p_2^*'s, and so on, we have the following set of sentences:

(19.6)

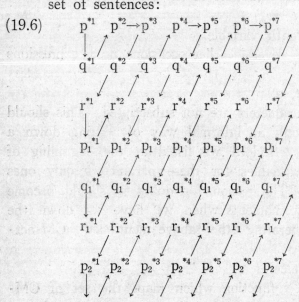

iv) Use diagonal method as indicated by the arrows in (19.6) to enumerate the sentences in (19.6). Denote this enumeration by

(19.7) $C_1, C_2, C_3...$

This is the desired enumeration of all (atomic) CM-act-sentences we mentioned above.

It may be noted in passing that this set of rules also provide an effective way to abbreviate any atomic CM-act-sentence to a starred sentence. For example, '$(x_1, t_2, w_3) p_{12}$' is abbreviated as 'p_{12}^{*2250}'.

So far we have taken into consideration only the CM-act-sentences in which the deontic terms are atomic. However, it is readily seen that every CM-act-sentence can be reduced to a CM-act-sentence with atomic deontic terms by (16.17) and (16.21) in § 16 together with the usual transformations among the truth-functional connectives. Hence, the procedure outlined above applies to any CM-act-proposition.

Next, we set up another mapping Ψ from the set of sentential variables p, q, r, p_1,...as given in the vocabulary for systems OT*—OS5* to the sentences in (19.7) in the following way

$$\Psi(p) = C_1, \qquad \Psi(q) = C_2, \qquad \Psi(r) = C_3,$$
$$\Psi(p_1) = C_4......$$

and so on.

We then transform a theorem, including the axioms, of OT* (OS4* or OS5*) to that of CMO_RT^* (CMO_RS4^* or CMO_RS5^*) in the following way:

$$S\frac{\text{`O', `p', `q', `r', `p_1',...}}{\text{`O}_R\text{', `}\Psi(p)\text{', `}\Psi(q)\text{', `}\Psi(r)\text{', `}\Psi(p_1)\text{',...}} \text{ (Thm)}$$

is a theorem of CMO_RT^* (CMO_RS4^* or CMO_RS5^*) provided that '(Thm)' is a theorem of OT* (OS4* or OS5*).

Furthermore, we may use the same numbering for theorems of these new CMO_R-systems as we did for O-systems. For example,

(OT*19) $\sim (Op \& O \sim p)$

is a theorem of OT*, then

(CMO_RT^*19) $\sim (O_R \Psi (p) \& O_R \sim \Psi (p))$

or

$$\sim (O_R C_1 \& O_R \sim C_1)$$

or

$$\sim (O_R p^{*1} \& O_R \sim p^{*1})$$

or

$$\sim (O_R p^{*30} \& \ O_R \sim p^{*30})$$

or finally

$$\sim (O_R (x_1, \ t_1, \ w_1) p \& O_R \sim (x_1, \ t_1, \ w_1) p)$$

is a theorem of CMO_RT^*, and so on. The results, then are three alternative deontic systems which are mapping images of our three previous systems.

Let us now compare these two different types of deontic logic. They are different in two significant respects: (1) the range of "deontic variables" or the operands of a deontic operator, and   (2) the deontic notions standing behind the symbols 'O' and 'O_R'. Although enough has been said about them in section 16 and section 17, some additional remarks on the second feature of difference seem desirable.

We may say that in the previous deontic systems, 'O' stands for our *total* notion of obligation which is backed up by the whole system of moralities of our society. However, it has been said in the last section that the system of moralities in our society is absolutely inconsistent.

Whether it is practically consistent remains to be seen. Hence, it may well be the case that our total notion of obligation is not a "consistent" notion. Thus, it is no wonder if we find that sometimes

$$Op \mathbin{\&} O \sim p$$

holds. This indeed is the core of trouble which accounts for the difficulties in Chisholm's dilemma and the dilemma of conflicting obligations.

Our new systems of deontic logic, on the other hand, formalize only a specific *partial* notion of obligation O_R which has a set R of moral rules standing in the background. And since we have agreed that R is a consistent set of moral rules, the following cannot be the case:

$$O_R p^* \mathbin{\&} O_R \sim p^*$$

This fact simply follows from the definition of the consistency of a set of moral rules.

Of course, if our whole system of moralities is consistent, our previous systems of deontic logic will be as good as the present systems in this respect. They may even be more desirable ones if we provide those systems with CM-act-sentences, for they formalize the total notion of obligation rather than a partial one.

§20. HINTIKKA-KRIPKE SEMANTICS FOR CMO T*—CMO$_R$S5*

We have so far outlined three alternative systems of deontic logic CMO$_R$T*, CMO$_R$S4* and CMO$_R$S5* and shown that they are, respectively, the mapping images of our earlier systems OT*, OS4* and OS5*. But, as we recall, we developed OT*—OS5* as axiomatic systems, and what we have for CMO$_R$T*—CMO$_R$S5* are likewise syntactical characterizations. In this section, we shall supplement them with semantical theories. The semantics we shall present is Hintikka's model set and model system with a minor modification in the manner of Kripke. [1]

First, we shall call a *deontic model set* any set μ of CM-act-formulas (sentence forms) which satisfies the following conditions:

(C20.1)   If A* $\in \mu$, then $\ulcorner \sim$A*$\urcorner \notin \mu$

(C20.2)   If $\ulcorner$[A* & B*]$\urcorner \in \mu$, then A* $\in \mu$ and B* $\in \mu$

(C20.3)   If $\ulcorner$[A* v B*]$\urcorner \in \mu$, then A* $\in \mu$ or B* $\in \mu$

Intuitively speaking, a deontic model set is a partial description of a possible world. It depicts only the portion of a world which has to do with human endeavorings (which are what CM-act-sentences are designed for).

---

1 See, for example, Hintikka [1963] and Kripke [1963]. Hintikka's method is applied to deontic logic in Hintikka [1957], Esperson [1967] and Åqvist [1967], while Kripke's method is applied to deontic logic in Hanson [1965].

Further, we let Ω be a non-empty set of deontic model sets defined above, and R be a binary relation defined on Ω. And we let ν be a member of Ω. We shall say that the orderd triple $\langle \Omega, \nu, R \rangle$ is a *deontic model system* if and only if the following conditions are satisfied:

(C20.4)   It is not the case that $\nu R \nu$

(C20.5)   For every $\mu \in \Omega$, there is at leat one μ^+ such that $\mu^+ R \mu$

(C20.6)   If $\ulcorner O_R A^* \urcorner \in \mu \in \Omega$, then $A^* \in \mu^+$ for every $\mu^+ \in \Omega$ such that $\mu^+ R \mu$

(C20.7)   If $\ulcorner P_R A^* \urcorner \in \mu \in \Omega$, then $A^* \in \mu^+$ for some $\mu^+ \in \Omega$ such that $\mu^+ R \mu$

The relation R above is called "copermissibility" by Hintikka and "deontic alternativeness" by Åqvist. [2] We shall follow Åqvist in saying that μ^+ is a *deontic alternative* to μ if $\mu^+ R \mu$ holds. Intuitively, we may think of μ^+ as a morally ideal world with respect to μ in the sense that what is obligatory in μ is actually the case in μ^+. And we may informally think of Ω as a set of possible worlds, and ν our actual world. To postulate the condition (C20.4) above is to say that the actual world is not a morally ideal world, because (D20.4) implies that there may be "some things" which ought to be done but are not actually done in ν. Now we say that a deontic model system is an OT* (*deontic*) *model system* if the follwing condition holds:

(C20.8) R is reflexive on Ω^*

where Ω^* is $\{\Omega\text{-}\nu\}$. It is an OS4* (*deontic*) *model system* if in addition to being an OT* model system, it also satisfies the following condition:

2 Hintikka [1957] and Åqvist [1967].

(C20.9) R is transitive on Ω

And finally a model system is an OS5* *model system* if it satisfies (C20.9) above and the following:

(C20.10)   If $\mu_1^+ R \mu$ and $\mu_2^+ R \mu$ then $\mu_1^+ R \mu_2^+$ for every μ, μ_1^+, μ_2^+

Next, we shall introduce the concepts of satisfiability and validity. We shall say that a set λ of CM-act-formulas is OT* (OS4*, OS5*) *satisfiable* if and only if there is an OT* (OS4*, OS5$^+$) model system $\langle \Omega, \nu, R \rangle$ such that λ is a subset of some member of Ω. [3] Now, a CM-act-formula A* is OT* (OS4*, OS5*) satisfiable if and only if the set {A*} having A* as its sole element is satisfiable. We say that A* is OT* (OS4*, OS5*) *contradictory* if and only if A* is not OT* (OS4*, OS5*) satisfiable. And, finally, we say that a CM-act-formula A* is OT* (OS4*, OS5*) *valid* if and only if $\ulcorner \sim A^* \urcorner$ is OT* (OS4*, OS5*) contradictory.

We shall not try to show that $CMO_R T^*$—$CMO_R S5^*$ are consistent and complete with respect to OT*—OS5* validity, respectively. However, as we shall apply this semantics in the next section to cope with a certain puzzle in deontic logic, namely Chisholm's dilemma, it seems desirable that we show how to determine that a formula is valid or contradictory by means of the model system. Let us do this by showing that the deontic axioms in $CMO_R T^*$—$CMO_R S5^*$ are, respectively, OT*—OS5* valid.

First, for the sake of simplicity, we shall put down the deontic axioms of $CMO_R T^*$ as follows:

---

3 Hintikka will say that λ is *imbeddable in* Ω.

(Ad*4) $\vdash O_R(p^* \supset q^*) \supset (O_R p^* \supset O_R q^*)$ [4]

(Ad*6) $\vdash O_R p^* \supset \sim O_R \sim p^*$

(Ad*7) $\vdash O_R((O_R p^*) \supset p^*)$

To show that (Ad*4) is OT* valid, we show that is negation is OT* contradictory. Suppose it is not contradictory, then there is at least one member μ of Ω in $\langle \Omega, \nu, R \rangle$ such that

$$O_R(p^* \supset q^*) \ \& \sim (O_R p^* \supset O_R q^*)$$

that is

$$O_R(\sim p^* \text{ v } q^*) \ \& \sim (\sim O_R p^* \text{ v } O_R q^*)$$

is a member of a subset of μ. By appealing to (C20.2) above, we have

$$O_R(\sim p^* \text{ v } q^*) \in \mu$$

and

$$\sim (\sim O_R p^* \text{ v } O_R q^*) \in \mu$$

i.e.,

$$(O_R p^* \ \& \sim O_R q^*) \in \mu$$

or

$$(O_R p^* \ \& \ P_R \sim q^*) \in \mu$$

That means, by (C20.2) again, we have the following:

(20.1) $O_R(\sim p^* \text{ v } q^*),\ O_R p^*,\ P_R \sim q^* \in \mu$

But according to (C20.7), since $P_R \sim q^* \in \mu$, there is at least one $\mu^+ \in \Omega$ such that $\mu^+ R \mu$, and

(20.2) $\sim q^* \in \mu^+$

And by (C20.6) and (20.1), since $O_R(\sim p^* \text{v } q^*),\ O_R p^* \in \mu$,

---

4 This is an informal way to write the axioms. According to what we have said in §19, we should have written (Ad*4) as

$$\vdash O_R[p^{*^{30}} \supset q^{*^{30}}] \supset [O_R p^{*^{30}} \supset O_R q^{*^{30}}]$$

or better as

$$\vdash O_R[\ (x_1,\ t_1,\ w_1)\,p \supset (x_1,\ t_1,\ w_1)\,q\,] \supset$$
$$[O_R(x_1,\ t_1,\ w_1)\,p \supset O_R(x_1,\ t_1,\ w_1)\,q]$$

we have the result that $(\sim p^* \vee q^*)$ and p^* are members of every μ_i^+ where $\mu_i^+ R \mu$. In particular, we have the following:

(20.3) $(\sim p^* \vee q^*),\ p^* \in \mu^+$

But by (C20.3) and (20.3) either $\sim p^* \in \mu^+$ or $q^* \in \mu$. If the first possibility, then this together with (20.3) implies that

(20.4) $p^* \in \mu^+$ and $\sim p^* \in \mu^+$

On the other hand, suppose that the second possibility holds, then this and (20.2) implies that

(20.5) $q^* \in \mu^+$ and $\sim q^* \in \mu^+$

In either case, we conclude that μ^+ is not a model set which contradicts our assumption that it is one (because $\mu^+ \in \Omega$). Therefore, the negation of (Ad*4) cannot be a member of (a subset of) an OT* model set. This in turn implies that the negation of (Ad*4) is OT* contradictory. Hence, (Ad*4) is OT* valid.

Likewise, we can easily show that (Ad*6) and (Ad*7) are OT* valid. To prove that (Ad*6) is OT* valid, use (C20.1)—(C20.3) and (C20.5)—(20.7). To prove (Ad*7) is OT* valid, use (C20.1)—(C20.3) (C20.5)—(C20.8).

It is easy to see that the above axioms are also OS4* valid. We may then show that the following axiom—which when added to the axioms above forms the axioms of $CMO_R S4^*$—is OS4* valid:

(Ad*8) $\vdash O_R p^* \supset O_R O_R p^*$

To see this, we apply the same procedure, showing that

(20.6) $\sim (O_R p^* \supset O_R O_R p^*)$

cannot be a member of a subset of a model set in an OS4* model system. It follows then that (20.6) is OS4* contradictory. That is, (Ad*8) is OS4* valid. The proof involves the essential uses of (C20.9).

Similarly, we may show that all the above axioms are OS5* valid. And it is also readily seen, by using (C20.10) among other things, that the following axiom which is the "characteristic axiom" of CMO_RS5^* is also OS5* valid:

(Ad*9) $\vdash \sim O_Rp^* \supset O_R \sim O_Rp^*$

§ 21. CHISHOLM'S DILEMMA, THE DILEMMA OF CONFLICTING OBLIGATIONS AND THE PARADOX OF THE GOOD SAMARITAN REVISITED

Now that we have exhibited alternative systems of deontic logic and pinpointed the troubles from which some of the deontic problems associated with the earlier systems of deontic logic come into being, let us now pay a renewed visit to what we have called Chisholm's dilemma, the dilemma of conflicting obligation, and the paradox of the Good Samaritan.

Chisholm's dilemma, as we recall, is a predicament to the following effect: [1] Certain systems of deontic logic are such that either they are unable to formulate contrary-to-duty imperative, or they contain a contradiction. Now, in our new systems, we want to show that the notion of contrary-to-duty imperative can be accounted for without running into a contradiction.

A contrary-to-duty imperative expressed in the earlier systems takes the following form:

(21.1)   One ought to do q.   (Oq)

and

(21.2)   One ought to do if-q-then-p. $(O(q \supset p))$

But

---

1 Cf. § 4.

(21.3)   If one does not do q, one ought to do not-p.
           $(\sim q \supset O \sim p)$

Now,

(21.4)   One does not do q. $(\sim q)$

Therefore,

(21.5)   One ought to do not-p. $(O \sim p)$

But, from (20.1) and (20.2) we have

(21.6)   One ought to do p. (Op)

Therefore, from (21.5) and (21.6), we get

(21.7)   One ought to do p and one ought to do not-p.
           $(Op$ & $O \sim p)$

However, there is a theorem in our previous system of deontic logic which reads:

(OT*19)   It is not the case that one ought to do p and
           one ought to do not-p. $(\sim (Op$ & $O \sim p))$

Finally, from (21.7) and (OT*19) we have a patent contradiction.

Now, in our present systems of deontic logic, we shall, for the time being, read the above argument in the following way:

(CM21.1)   One, say x_1, ought to bring it about that q at
           t_1 in w_1 $(O_R (x_1, t_1, w_1) q)$

and

(CM21.2)   One ought to bring it about that if-q-then-p at
           t_1 in w_1.
           $(O_R (x_1, t_1, w_1)(q \supset p))$

(CM21.3)   If one does not bring it about that q at t_1 in
           w_1, then one ought to bring it about that not-p
           at t_1 in w_1.
           $(\sim (x_1, t_1, w_1) q \supset O_R (x_1, t_1, w_1) \sim p)$

Now,

(CM21.4)   One does not bring it about that q at t_1 in w_1.

$\qquad$ $(\sim (x_1,\ t_1,\ w_1)\,q)$

Therefore,

(CM21.5)   One ought to bring it about that not-p at t_1 in w_1.

$\qquad$ $(O_R\,(x_1,\ t_1,\ w_1)\,\sim p)$

Indeed, from (CM21.1) and (CM21.2), we can derive

(CM21.6)   One ought to bring it about that p at t_1 in w_1.

$\qquad$ $(O_R\,(x_1,\ t_1,\ w_1)\,p)$

Because ' $(x_1,t_1,w_1)(q \supset p)$ ', as we mentioned before, has the same truth condition as ' $(x_1,\ t_1,\ w_1)\,q \supset (x_1,\ t_1,\ w_1)\,p$ ', and because

$$O_R\,(x_1,\ t_1,\ w_1)\,q\ \&\ O_R[\,(x_1,\ t_1,\ w_1)\,q \supset (x_1,\ t_1,\ w_1)\,p\,]$$
$$\supset O_R\,(x_1,\ t_1,\ w_1)\,p$$

is a variant theorem of $(CMO_R T^*35)$. And from (CM21.5) and (CM21.6) we have

(CM21.7)   One ought to bring it about that p at t_1 in w_1, and one ought to bring it about that not-p at t_1 in w_1.

$\qquad$ $(O_R\,(x_1,\ t_1,\ w_1)\ \&\ O_R\,(x_1,\ t_1,\ w_1)\,\sim p)$

which when abbreviated is

(CM21.8) $O_R p^{*^{30}}\ \&\ O_R \sim p^{*^{30}}$

But

$(CMO_R T^*19)$ $\quad \sim (O_R p^{*^{30}}\ \&\ O_R \sim p^{*^{30}})$

is a theorem of our new system (s). Hence, a contradiction.

Let us now look into the trouble by examining some of the possible exits out of this difficulty.

First, it may be argued that there is some undesirable logical reasoning involved in the generating of the above contradiction. In particular, people might want to argue against the derivation from $O_R\,(x_1,\ t_1,\ w_1)\,q$ and $O_R\,(\,(x_1,$

$t_1,\ w_1)\,\mathrm{q} \supset (x_1,\ t_1,\ w_1)\,\mathrm{p})$ to $\mathrm{O_R}\,(x_1,\ t_1,\ w_1)\,\mathrm{p}$, having in mind that a set of moral rules R may require $(x_1,\ t_1,\ w_1)\,\mathrm{q}$ and $(x_1,\ t_1,\ w_1)\,\mathrm{q} \supset (x_1,\ t_1,\ w_1)\,\mathrm{p}$ but fail to require $(x_1,\ t_1,\ w_1)\,\mathrm{p}$. Indeed, given that B is a logical consequence of A, R may require A without requiring B. Hence A may be obligatory but B may not. However, we shall not take this as a proper way to escape our present difficulty, because this will upset our deontic systems—to be sure, any deontic system we have seen so far—to a great extent, and force us to construct a deontic system anew.

A second alternative to escape the above difficulty could be this. Since the assumption that our morality admits of the restorative course of action leads to a contradiction, hence, by *reductio ad absurdum*, our assumption cannot be true. That is, our morality allows no such restitution. Again, this approach will be dismissed without any further ado, because this seems only to throw away the baby with the bath water, for we have said early in the last chapter that reparative course of action is desirable.

The third and last alternative we shall consider, and indeed the one we favor, is to differentiate several levels of obligation within a morality. When we say rule R requires that p^{*30}, we mean, according to our earlier definition, that p^{*30} is obligatory, or in short

$$\mathrm{O_R p}^{*30}$$

We shall call this obligation a *primary* obligation. After we fail to fulfill our primary obligation, the moral rule R may require that we do $\sim\mathrm{p}^{*30}$ as restitution or reparation. This will be called a *secondary* obligation, and will be symbolized as

$$\mathrm{O'_R} \sim \mathrm{p}^{*30}$$

Indeed we may have, as we suggested in Chapter One, further levels of restoration, and hence, further levels of obligation: *tertiary* obligation, *quaternary* obligation,..., n-*ary* obligation, each is introduced only after the preceding one fails to be accomplished. We shall symbolize them, respectively, by

$$O''_R, \; O'''_R, ..., \; O\overbrace{'''_R...}^{n-1}\!'$$

After different levels of obligation are introduced, we shall stipulate a meta-moral rule to prescribe how different levels of obligation are in force. The meta-fule is:

(M21.1)   If a primary obligation and a secondary obligation are in conflict, the primary obligation is in force. If the primary obligation, for some reason or other, cannot be fulfilled, the secondary obligation is in effect. In this case, the primary obligation ceases to be in force.

This seems a plausible rule indeed, because, as we mentioned above, it is only after the primary obligation fails to be accomplished that the secondary obligation goes into effect. Thus, at the time the secondary obligation takes effect the fulfillment of the primary obligation is already out of question. The primary obligation is no longer in effect.

Now, the difficulty which Chisholm pointed out does not threaten our present system of deontic logic in the same way as it did the former system. For we now only have

(CM21.8′) $O_R p^{*30}$ & $O'_R \sim p^{*30}$

rather than (CM21.8) above. Therefore, we do not have a contradiction.

We may note that in the case of $(CM21.8')$, p^{*30} is a primary obligation prescribed by R, (but since it fails to be fulfilled for some reason or other), R then prescribes $\sim p^{*30}$ as a secondary obligation. According to $(M21.1)$, only this secondary obligation, not together with the primary one, is now in effect.

Of course this does not mean that a man can escape his (primary) duty by shifting to an obligation of a lower level. An unfulfilled primary duty is still left unfulfilled. A reparative secondary obligation, for example, gives one a chance for compensation, it does not offer one a moral escape.

This seems indeed a proper way, if not the proper way, to get ourselves out of the contradiction. For the primary obligation and (different levels of) the so-called contrary-to-duty imperatives, or, contrary-to-duty obligations, as we prefer to call them in this case, are not in force at the same time. A secondary contrary-to-duty obligation is in force only if the accomplishment of the primary obligation is no longer to be considered; in general, an n-ary contrary-to-duty obligation is not in effect unless the primary obligation, the secondary obligation, and...and the n-1-ary contrary-to-duty obligation are all out of the question.

However, it is immediately seen that $(CM21.8')$ above is not expressible in our present systems of deontic logic. But we may try to extend our systems to incorporate different levels of obligations in such a way that $(CMO_R T^*19)$ and

$(CM21.9)$ $\sim (O'_R p^{*30} \ \& \ O'_R \sim p^{*30})$

and, in general,

$$(\sim O_R' \overbrace{\dots}^{n} 'p^{*30} \ \& \ O_R' \overbrace{\dots}^{n} '\sim p^{*30})$$

are all theorems, but (CM21.8) above is not.

At this point we find that in one of his recent articles, Åqvist expresses the same idea of differentiating levels of obligation.[2] His solution to Chisholm's puzzle is similar to what we proposed above and thus can be readily transferred to our systems.

In the last section we spelt out the semantics for our present systems of deontic logic $CMO_R T^*$-$CMO_R S5^*$. But, as we recall, we have coped only with a deontic operator 'O_R' (and the corresponding 'P_R'). Now, since we want to talk about a lower level of obligation, we shall introduce another deontic operator 'O'_R'(and the corresponding 'P'_R'). Here we may take '$O_R p^*$' as saying that p^* is a primary obligation, or that p^* is primarily obligatory; and '$O'_R p^*$' as saying that p^* is a secondary obligation, or that p^* is secondarily obligatory. With this introduction of an additional deontic operator 'O'_R' we need then to make some corresponding adjustments in the semantics.

Let us call the systems resulting from adding 'O'_R' to $CMO_R T^*$—$CMO_R S5^*$ (and also the other necessary amendments) $CMO_R T^{*+}$—$CMO_R S5^{*+}$, respectively. Now for these "extended" systems, we have the same notion of model set as we defined in the last section. But we want to specify another relation in addition to R (the deontic alternativeness) of the last section in order to bring to light the relationship between the primary and the secondary obligations. We denote this new relation by 'R^0' and call

---

[2] See Åqvist [1967].

it *compensatory deontic alternativeness.* We shall read
'$\mu'R^0\mu$' as 'μ' is compensatorily alternative to μ'. [3] We shall
further stipulate that O'_R, P'_R, and R^0 have the corresponding properties postulated in (C20.4)—(C20.7).

An OT*+(OS4*+, OS5*+) model system will then be
defined as an ordered quadruple $\langle \Omega, \nu, R, R^0 \rangle$ (where 'Ω',
'ν' and 'R' are the same as defined in the last section)
such that the following additional condition holds: [4]

(C21.1)   If $O_R A^*$, $B^* \in \mu \in \Omega$ and $\mu'R^0\mu$ where $\mu' \in \Omega$
and B^* is truth functionally incompatible with
A^*, then $B^* \in \mu'$

In addition, OT*+(OS4*+, OS5*+) satisfiability and validity
are defined in the manner parallel to the definitions in the
last section.

It may be observed that the condition (C21.1) war-
rants, roughly speaking, that the violation of a (primary)
obligation can be compensated in a compensatory deontic
world as a (secondary) obligation. We can see that this
immediately gives us a way out of Chisholm's puzzle.

As we have said above, what is said to be the Chisholm's puzzle is not a genuine contradiction, but one
which looks like the following:

(CM21.8′) $O_R p^{*^{30}}$ & $O'_R \sim p^{*^{30}}$

But now it is easily seen that (CM21.8′) is not a contradiction in either of the systems $CMO_R T^{*+}$—$CMO_R S5^{*+}$.
That is, we can show that (CM21.8′) is OT*+ (also OS4*+

---

3 Åqvist calls R^0 "perfect deontic alternativeness" and read '$\mu'R^0\mu$'
  as 'μ' is an ideal extension of μ'. *Ibid.*

4 Åqvist has an ordered triple $\langle \Omega, R, R^0 \rangle$ in this case. But this
  model system fails to further distinguish between an OT*+ model
  system, an OS4*+ model system and an OS5*+ model system.

and OS5*$^+$) satisfiable. The following model system Ω suffices to show the desired result:

$$\Omega = \{\mu, \ \mu^+, \ \mu'\}$$
$$R = \{<\mu^+, \ \mu>\}$$
$$R^0 = \{<\mu', \ \mu>\}$$

$$\mu' < \!\!\!-\!\!\!-\!\!\!-\!\!\!R^0\!\!\!-\!\!\!-\!\!\!-\!\!\!-\!\!\!\mu\!\!\!-\!\!\!-\!\!\!-\!\!\!-\!\!\!R\!\!\!-\!\!\!-\!\!\!-\!\!\!> \mu^+$$
$$\sim p^{*30} \qquad O_R p^{*30} \ \& \ O'_R \sim p^{*30} \qquad p^{*30}$$
$$O_R p^{*30}$$
$$O'_R \sim p^{30}$$

Next, we shall observe how our new systems shed fresh light on the dilemma of conflicting obligations. This dilemma can be briefly stated as follows. In some systems of deontic logic, either it is impossible to express the notion of "conflicting obligations" adequately, or else, they contain a contradiction. [5]

"Conflicting obligations" is a situation in which we are obliged to do several mutually incompatible acts, in particular, a certain act and its negation. Or, in symbols,

$$Op \ \& \ O \sim p$$

It is evident from what we have arrived at in the last section that no single set of moral rules R will oblige one to do something and its negation, because every set of moral rules is consistent. That is to say,

(21.9) $O_R p^* \ \& \ O_R \sim p^*$

is always false for every O_R. [6] A conflict of duties can only happen when one submits oneself to incompatible moralities simultaneously, and hence there comes the moral

---

5 Cf. section 15.

6 We shall again use the unsuperscripted 'p*' etc. on the occasion when no confusion seems likely.

predicament. That is, the following might be true:

(21.11) $O_Rp^* \& O_{R'}\sim p^*$

where $R \neq R'$. But this is not a contradiction in our systems of deontic logic. Of course, (21.11) is again not even expressible in our new systems.

However one might again try to think of extending our systems in such a way—adding, among other things, an additional deontic operator 'O_R' to join the 'O_R' we already have—that will accommodate expressions like (21. 11). If this extension is carried out, then whether the resulting systems contain a contradiction or not, depends upon (i) whether we have meta-rules which direct over-ruling relation among different moralities, and (ii) what is the actual direction these overruling rules give. It might be the case that we shall have a rule to the following effect:

(21.12)   If O_R and $O_{R'}$ are incompatible and O_Rp^* and $O_{R'}\sim p^*$, then there is an $O_{R''}$ which overrules O_R and $O_{R'}$, and $O_{R''}q^*$ (or $F_{R''}q^*$ or $I_{R''}q^*$).

where q^* may be either p^* or $\sim p^*$.

In this case, the conflicting obligations (i.e., between obligation and obligation') is settled. They are replaced by another new obligation (i.e., obligation''). This is a situa-tion which comes very close to Ross' conception of finding the actual duty when there are conflicting *prima-facie* obligations.

But it might also happen that there is no other $O_{R''}$ which will overrule O_R and $O_{R'}$; but these two are still incompatible and are no longer overruled by any other morality. In this case, our system is practically inconsistent. Conflicting obligation is a genuine unsolvable problem in this case. However, it should be realized that this problem comes, as we showed in the last section, from the inconsistency of our system of molralities. It does not come from any inadequacy in our deontic logic.

We come now to the paradox of the Good Samaritan. The following may be thought of as one of the possible solutions.

First, we know that this paradox comes from the fact that we allow the following "principle" to hold:

(21.13)   What entails a forbidden act is itself forbidden.

or

(OM28) $(Fp \mathbin{\&} q \mathbin{\dashv} p) \supset Fq$ [7]

However, (21.13) in our present systems demands a careful reformulation. We shall propose the following:

(21.14)   What entails a subsequent forbidden act is itself forbidden.

Or, in our terminology,

(21.15) $[F_R (x_2, \, t_2, \, w_2) \, p \mathbin{\&}. \, (x_1, \, t_1, \, w_1) \, q \mathbin{\dashv} (x_2, \, t_2, \, w_2) \, p]$
$\supset F_R (x_1, \, t_1, \, w_1) \, q. \mathbin{\&} \, G \, t_1 t_2$

where x_1, w_1 may be the same, respectively, as x_2, w_2, and '$G_{①②}$' means ② comes after ①.

It is clear, then, that the Good Samaritan did not do something forbidden by helping the victim of robbery, because to help a victim of robbery does not entail that a subsequent robbery occurs.

That is to say, if we extend our systems by including alethic modalities and some predicate symbols, in particular '$G_{①②}$' we shall reject (OM28) of Anderson in favor of (21.15).

---

7 See § 13.

Of course, we do not claim that this is the only way to overcome or bypass the paradox of the Good Samaritan. Perhaps the concept of "entailment" is simply too strong for deontic logic in that situation.

§ 22. QUANTIFIERS AND ALETHIC MODALITIES IN DEONTIC LOGIC

Since we have confined ourselves to propositional deontic logic, the problem of quantifiers lies outside the scope of our discussion. However, after we have observed the present type of deontic logic, the introduction of quantifiers seems a natural step of further development. Hence, this section seems a reasonable place for us to briefly discuss the matter. We shall also briefly review, in the latter half of this section, the problems which arise when we incorporate alethic modalities into deontic logic.

As we recall, a CM-act-sentence in the new systems of deontic logic has the following logical form:

(22.1) x at t in w brings it about that p.

or, in our symbolism,

(22.2) (x, t, w)p

which contains four different kinds of "individual" variables. It is easily seen that each of these variables can be quantified. For instance, we may write down a quantified sentence like

(22.3)   For any man at any time in any place there is some act which the man brings about.

This is an awkward logical version of the following more natural sentence.

(22.4)   Every man brings about some act at any time in any place.

which is, in our symbolism,

(22.5) $(x)(t)(w)(\exists p)((x,\, t,\, w)p)$

Hence, we have at least four different types of variables for a quantifier to bind. But this is hardly the end of the story. Consider the following formula:

(22.6) $(x)(t)(w)(p)\ [O_R(x,\, t,\, w)p \supset$
             $\sim O_R \sim (x,\, t,\, w)p]$

or

(22.7) $(x)(t)(w)(p)[O_R(x,\, t,\, w)p \supset P_R\ (x,\, t,\, w)p]$

That is,

(22.8)   At any time in any place, if anyone ought to bring about any act, then he is permitted to bring about that act at that time in that place.

In (22.6) we see that 'O_R' occurs as a free variable. But it can also be quantified. Thus, we may write

(22.9) $(O_R)(x)(t)(w)(p)[O_R(x,\, t,\, w)p \supset$
             $\sim O_R \sim (x,\, t,\, w)p]$

That is,

(22.10)   In any sense of 'ought', if anyone at any time in any place ought to bring about an act, then in the related sense of 'permission', he is permitted to bring about that act at that time in that place.

Here, 'related sense of 'permission'' can be defined as "the same sense of not-ought-not". Because the following formula holds:

(22.11) $(O_R)(P_R)(p^*)(P_R p^* \equiv\, \sim O_R \sim p^*)$

Of course (22.11) is only an abbreviation for a formula in our language. It is not itself a formula in that language.

Let us call a quantified deontic system which puts only those four kinds of individual variables under the scope of a quantifier, *first-order deontic logic*. If a deontic operator, in particular 'O_R', is also brought into the range of quantification, then we call the system *second-order deontic logic.*

The significance of quantifiers in deontic logic is readily appreciated. Deontic logic may be used to formalize ethical norms. Now, norms must be expressed in general terms which speak of all cases or at least some cases. For instance, one of the Islamic norms might be this.

(22.12)　　One ought to go to Mecca to worship God at a particular time of the year.

This certainly can only be satisfactorily expressed in first-order deontic logic. We may propose to write it as follows:

(22.13)　　$(x)(\exists t)(\exists w)(\exists p)(w = \text{Mecca} \,\&\, p = $ to worship the God $\&\, O(x, t, w)p)$

Another example. We may wish to express in our deontic logic the following statement:

(22.14)　　If a set R_i of rules obliges a man x_1 at t_1 in w_1 to bring about p, and another set R_j of rules obliges him at t_1 in w_1 to bring about $\sim$p, then, there is a further set R_k of rules which overrules R_i and R_j and which obliges him at t_1 in w_1 to bring about q (where q is either p or $\sim$p).

This may be expressed as a formula in second-order deontic logic as follows.

(22.15)　　$(O_{R_i})(O_{R_j})(x_1)(t_1)(w_1)(p)\,[(O_{R_i}(x_1, t_1, w_1)p \,\&\,$
$O_{R_j}(x_1, t_1, w_1)\sim p) \supset (O_{R_k})(O_{R_k}$ overrules O_{R_i}
and $O_{R_j} \,\&\, O_{R_k}(x_1, t_1, w_1)q) \,\&\, (q = p \lor q = \sim p)]$

It seems obvious that an investigation into second-order deontic logic is not only desirable but essential if we want really to cope with certain important deontic problems such as the dilemma of conflicting obligations. The reason is that the morality which we intuitively conceived might not be a clear-cut and homogeneous thing. It seems more appropriate to think of our system of moralities as a mixture of moral rules of different levels. That is, moralities mingle with meta-moralities. We seem not only to have moral rules but also to have meta-moral rules in our moralities. For instance, the following looks more like a meta-moral rule than a moral rule.

(22.16)   When different goods are compared, have the greatest; when several evils are present, take the smallest. (Motze)

Likewise, we may find the following rule being enforced in our morality.

(22.17)   Abandon your "partisan" duties, give way to altruistic obligations.

This, again, seems to be a meta-moral rule rather than a moral rule. These rules, roughly speaking, tell us which morality overrules which others.

Therefore, if it is true that our system of moralities is one in which moralities are mixed up with meta-moralities, then it is indispensable to make a survey of second-order deontic logic provided that we want to get a complete view of the whole story of our morality. Only in second-order deontic logic can the problem of meta-moralities be fully formulated and satisfactorily handled.

Next we come to the problems of alethic modalities in deontic logic. We shall discuss the problems by concentrating our attention on certain particular examples. First, the so-called Kantian principle that what I ought to do I can do.

As we have seen in § 13, this principle appears as a theorem of Anderson's systems OM—OM″ in the following form:

(OM24) $Op \supset \diamondsuit p$

A natural question now arises: What kind of possibility do we have in mind when we use '$\diamondsuit$' to refer to it? Can it be *logical possibility* ('$\diamondsuit^l$'), *empirical possibility* ('$\diamondsuit^e$'), *technical possibility* ('$\diamondsuit^t$') ' or *personal possibility* ('$\diamondsuit^p$')?

We will not try to give a precise definition of each of the above four notions of possibility. Suffice it to say that personal possibility entails technical possibility, technical possibility entails empirical possibility and empirical possibility, in turn, entails logical possibility. Hence, (OM24) will be a strongest thesis if '$\diamondsuit$' means personal possibility; and weakest, if '$\diamondsuit$' means logical possibility, with the other two alternatives standing in between in the order of strength if '$\diamondsuit$' means technical possibility and empirical possibility, respectively.

The difficulty associated with the Kantian principle is twofold. First, the distinction between the possible and the impossible is not clear-cut. The demarcation line is subject to change. This is true even in the case in which what we mean by possibility is the logical one. Simply reflect on the fact that the class of logical laws does not seem to be well-defined and determinable once and for all. Fortunately, this difficulty seems to be a minor one. Once we realize that the distinction is not clear and distinct, we can proceed with the necessary precaution to draw a most desirable line.

The second difficulty, on the other hand, seems more formidable. The difficulty is this: it seems that what we expect as the Kantian principle is not the weakest version of (OM24), namely, to interpret '$\diamondsuit$' as logical possibility.

When we say that what one ought to do one can do, we seem to mean at least a stronger version intending '◇' to refer to empirical possibility, or technical possibility, or even personal possibility. Indeed it is completely natural if a person claims that what he means by the Kantian principle is this:

(22.8)   What one ought to do one can do within one's power, i.e., in one's personal possibility.

That is

(22.9) $Op \supset \diamondsuit^{p}p$

However, when we allow the Kantian principle to take a stronger form, it may no longer hold. Let us consider here the strongest version of this principle, namely (22.9). The other two versions can be discussed in a similar vein.

We may ask the following question: Does it ever happen that a person ought to do something which he has no ability to do? Obviously, there are lots of examples. I may be obliged to pay my debt but at the time when the payment is due I have no money to pay. Or, I might be under an obligation to keep my office hours, but I was delayed by an unexpected traffic jam, and so on. The examples can easily be multiplied *ad nauseam*. (22.19) seems, in a word, greatly to go against our intuition.

The uncertainty about the Kantian principle also accounts for part of the reason why it seems highly desirable to allow reparative efforts in our morality. [1]

Next, we are going to examine the following two theorems of Anderson's OM—OM''.

(OM21) $\square p \supset Op$

---

[1] Cf. § 4 and see note 3 of that section.

and

(OM23) $\sim \diamondsuit p \supset Fp$

Again there is all the ambiguity concerning the meaning of '$\diamondsuit$' (or '$\square$'), again there are different versions of these theorems, each of them having different degrees of strength. And again, when we take the stronger versions of them, they seem at best dubious, if not flatly false.

And to make things even worse, let us remind ourselves that there might be a principle or a meta-rule in our morality to the following effect:

(22.20)   What one ought to do, one ought to *try;* what one is forbidden to do, one must *not* try.

Indeed this seems to be a reasonable principle, because it is not only the actual performance, but also the attempt to perform which counts in a moral evaluation. For example, there is a great difference between total non-performance and having attempted but failed. However, once (22.20) is agreed upon, we immediately find ourselves drived to the wall.

Consider (OM23). It says that what is impossible must not be done (is forbidden to be done). By (22.20), we have:

(22.21)   What is impossible must not be attempted.

This, of course, is intolerable as a thesis in deontic logic even if we take 'possibility' to mean the most unproblematic one, namely, logical possibility. For (22.21) implies, among other things, that those mathematicians who tried to prove the dependnece of the parallel postulate on the other Euclidean postulates, or those who tried to trisect an arbitrary angle with only a straightedge and compass; or the logicians who attempted to find a general decision procedure for first-order logic, or those who attempted to show the consistency and completeness of first-order arithmetic, committed a certain kind of moral error! [2] It follows that those who claim that (OM21) and (OM23) are harmlessly acceptable in deontic logic, because of the fact that logically necessary acts are automatically done and logically impossible acts cannot be performed anyway, seem to make a mistake. For while they make a detour to avoid the original difficulty they will find themselves unwittingly stepping into another pitfall nearby.

---

[2] And things become even more astonishing if we allow '◇' to designate other kinds of possibility.

CHAPTER THREE

MORAL USES OF LANGUAGE
AND IMPERATIVE LOGIC

§ 23. DUAL FUNCTIONS OF LANGUAGE IN A MORAL CONTEXT: EVALUATION AND DIRECTION

As we indicated in § 15, some criticisms of imperative logic have been taken to be applicable *mutatis mutandis* to deontic logic. Consciously or not, this is done however with good reason. As we shall see in this chapter, a system of deontic logic and the *corresponding* system of imperative logic may be regarded as isomorphic models of the same theory. [1] The justification of the relationship between the deontic model and the imperative model lies in the fact that in a moral context a language, as a rule, assumes two functions: *evaluation* and *direction*. A sentence in such a context can be used, on the one hand, to grade, to set up maxims, or to evaluate; it can, on the other hand, be used to order, to command, or to direct action. Let us call the former uses of language *evaluative*, and the latter uses *directive*.

In a moral context, these two uses of language have a close relationship to each other. What this relationship is exactly, we shall try to spell out later.

Meanwhile, some preliminary remarks are called for. First, by 'imperative logic' we mean, in this discussion, the

---

1 The phrase 'the corresponding system of imperative logic' will become clear as we proceed. See, especially, §§ 25-26 below.

logic of commands in its more restricted sense. We may call it the logic of *moral* commands. Just as deontic logic may be understood either in a wider or less restricted sense as the logic of obligation in general, or, as the common practice goes, in a narrower or more restricted sense as the logic of moral obligation; so too imperative logic can be construed either in a less restricted sense as the logic of commands in general, or in a restricted sense, as we proposed above. It is in the narrower sense that we are going to use the terms 'deontic logic' and 'imperative logic'. It is also in this sense that we maintain that deontic logic and imperative logic are really two sides of the same coin. They are mirror images of each other. 2

The second point we want to make clear before we take up the discussion of pragmatics is this. We shall take it to be the case that there are two distinguishable, though not necessarily separable, theories of morality. We have, on the one hand, a theory of (moral) *value*, and, on the other hand, a theory of (moral) *duty*. The notions which we commonly encounter in the former are "goodness", "badness", "ideal", "value", and so on; while that which we usually find in the latter are "obligation", "permission", "duty", and the like. For the sake of facilitating our discussion, we shall reconstruct these two theories in the following way.

We shall consider a theory of value as a depiction of a morally ideal world or a description of a morally best

---

2 Although we have devoted ourselves only to the restricted sense of deontic logic and imperative logic, it is easy to see that general deontic logic and imperative logic are nothing but simple semantical extensions of the former.

possible world. Let T_i be such a theory of value, and W_i be the ideal world it depicts. We shall regard as *a basic moral sentence* in a theory of value any expression of the following form:

(23.1)   It is desirable[i] that p.

or, in symbols

(23.2) $D_{T_i}p$

where p is a certain proposition (or state of affairs), not necessarily an act-proposition. And 'desirable[i]' means "desirable according to the theory of value T_i." Indeed, (23.1) can, then, be defined as

(23.3)   p is a true proposition (or state of affairs) in W_i

That is,

(D22.4) $D_{T_i}p =_{Df} p \in W_i$

provided that we let the *definiens* mean (23.3). A world is considered simply as a collection of propositions or states of affairs.

Similarly, we may, in agreement with what we have said in Chapter Two (§ 17 in particular), think of a theory of duty as a collection of (moral) rules. Let R_i be a particular theory of duty, that is, a set of (moral) rules. The following, then, is an example of a typical moral sentence in it.

It is required[i] that p*.

i.e.,

(23.5) R_i requires that p*. [3]

or, in symbols

(23.6) $R_i p^*$

where 'p*', as in the last chapter, 'stands for a CM-act-

---

[3] Cf. (D17.1) in § 17.

proposition.

It may be mentioned that there is a certain relation holding between a theory of value and a theory of duty. What exactly this relation is, we shall, nevertheless, not try to investigate or specify here; it lies beyond the scope of our discussion. Suffice it to say that, more often than not, a theory of value "yields" at least one theory of duty. On the contrary, a theory of duty usually "presupposes" a certain theory of value. Besides, a theory of value may be thought of as expressing a certain maximum or ultimate expectation, while a theory of duty, in contrast, may be thought of as voicing a certain minimum or least require-ment. Of course, all these statements are vague. But since we are not in a position to make a closer scrutiny of this topic, we let them stand as vaguely as they are, serving not as a precise characterization, but merely as a rough in-dication or suggestion.

We now turn our attention to the main concern of this section: pragmatics of moral uses of language. We shall maintain, from the beginning, that when we utter

(23.1)   It is desirable[i] that p.

We intend it to serve the same purpose (s) as the utterance of

(23.7)   p is good[i].

together with, although perhaps not with the same degree of emphasis as, the utterance of

(23.8)   Do your best to bring p about![i]

Here, again, the superscript 'i' in (23.7) and (23.8), as it does in (23.1), refers us back to the theory T_i. If we use '$G_{T_i}p$' to symbolize 'p is good[i]', and '$(\Diamond !_{T_i}) p$' to symbolize 'Do your best to bring p about[i]', then what we try to maintain is that the purpose (s) we try to achieve by uttering

(23.2) $D_T\, p$

is the same as the combined (in a certain manner) purpose (s) we try to achieve by uttering

(23.9) $G_{T_i} p$

and

(23.10) $(\diamondsuit !\, _{T_i})\, p$

We may note that (23.7) or (23.9) is used characteristically to evaluate and (23.8) or (23.10) is used characteristically to direct action. It is our proposal that (23.1) or (23.2) be employed to fulfill both of these two purposes. In short, they perform a dual-function of language: evaluation and direction, making value judgments and directing action.

The issue in question may be explained more clearly in terms of the pragmatic theory of meaning proposed and developed by Henry S. Leonard. [4] According to Leonard, the purpose of an author in uttering a sentence can be analyzed into a *concern* and a *topic of concern*. Roughly speaking, the concern of a purpose is what the author wishes to accomplish, and the topic of concern is "that proposition relative to which he has this concern." [5] Here, the word 'proposition' is understood in the same sense as we understood it in the last chapter, as a state of affairs.

---

4 See Leonard [1957] or [1967], unit 14. However, we do not mean to say, as Leonard seems to imply, that pragmatic considerations can be used to fully characterize meaning. (See *ibid.*, § 14.3: Meaning as purpose). On this point, see Hsiu-hwang Ho, "The Pragmatic Concept of Translation" (to appear)

5 Leonard, *ibid.*

Before we set out to give examples, let us remind ourselves that moral value judgments are *impersonal evaluations,* and moral commands are *impersonal imperatives.* When x, addressing y, says: 'It is obligatory[i] that you go to fight in Vietnam', it is the set of moral rules R_i, not x, that are claimed to prescribe that y goes to fight in Vietnam. The utterance made by x serves to remind y or to let y know that R_i makes such a prescription. Similar remarks hold for moral commands. However, if we like, we might think of x in the above situation as a mouthpiece of, or as a spokesman for, or a *locum tenens* of, the moral rules R_i when he makes moral value-judgments or issues moral commands. Thus, the distinction between personal and impersonal evaluations or imperatives becomes rather unnecessary. [6]   In either case, it is all-important to keep in mind that, in our discussion, moral judgments and moral commands are always backed up by a set of moral rules. Our uses of 'moral obligation' and 'moral imperative' are understood similarly. It is with regard to this kind of moral obligations that our deontic logic is said to be a logic of (moral) obligation; likewise, it is this kind of moral imperatives that we try to formalize in our imperative logic.

Let us now examine briefly how the Leonardian analysis can apply to moral sentences. First, moral sentences in the so-called theory of value.

Suppose a person x says:

(23.11)   It is good[i] for y to be friendly.

In uttering this sentence, x, acting as a mouthpiece of a certain ethical theory T_i, grades or evaluates as good that

_____

[6] Cf. Leonard [1959], p. 185.

y be friendly. Here, "to grade or evaluate as good (that...)" is the concern, and "that y be friendly" is the topic of concern, of x's uttering the sentence (23.11). Since x's concern in this case is to grade or to evaluate, we shall call the concern an *evaluative* one. And since the purpose of uttering a sentence (by a person), according to Leonard, consists of a concern and a topic of concern, we shall also call the purpose of uttering (23.11) an *evaluative purpose*. Language when used for an evaluative purpose is said to have an *evaluative function*. (23.11) then, exemplifies the evaluative function of language.

Similarly, when x in addressing y says:

(23.12)   Do your best to be friendly![i].

the concern is (again acting as a mouthpiece of T_i) "to command, or to direct, y to do his best to bring it about or to make it true (that...)", and the topic of concern is, again, "that y be friendly". likewise, since the concern is to command or to direct someone to bring about some state of affairs, we shall call it a *directive* concern. We shall also say that (23.12) serves a *directive purpose*, or that the language used in (23.12) has a *directive function*. (23.12) above exemplifies the directive function of language.

It may be remarked that the same sentence may be used to serve different purposes. For example, when x says:

(23.13)   It is raining.

He may want to report a "fact", or he may want to tell a lie. He may use (23.13) to suggest to someone who is going out to bring an umbrella with him. Or he may even utter this sentence as a joke when he sees someone polishing his car. These, and conceivably many others, are different functions which (23.13) may be used to serve.

However, a sentence standing in a certain context usually has a *characteristic* use or function. Under normal conditions, for example, in the radio weather broadcast, (23.13) is used, as a rule, to report a fact to, rather than to play a joke on, the listeners.

In the same manner, when we say that (23.11) above has an evaluative function, we mean that that sentence has evaluative function as its characteristic use in a normal moral situation. As a matter of fact, (23.11) may have other uses, e.g., directive use or other practical uses, provided the speaker so intends. A similar remark holds for (23.12). The sentence (23.12) exemplifies, as its characteristic use in a normal moral situation, a directive function of language, but it could well be used otherwise under other conditions.

In what follows, when we talk about the function of a sentence, we mean its characteristic use in a certain context explicitly spelt out or otherwise understood.

We shall next come to see the relationship between the evaluative function and the directive function of language used in a moral context. In particular, we shall exhibit the relationship between a moral sentence like (23.11) serving an evaluative function and another moral sentence like (23.12) serving a directive function. This relationship can be put in the following way.

Suppose x, acting as the mouthpiece of theory T_i (henceforth the same condition is assumed without explicit mention), speaks to y thus:

(23.14)   It is good for you to be friendly.

and goes on saying that he does not command (or advise, etc.) y to do his best to be friendly, that is, denies that he would make the following command:

(23.15)   Do your best to be friendly!

Then, there is an "inconsistency" of a certain kind involved. This kind of inconsistency is to be explained as follows. In a moral context, when a man, speaking for a theory of value T_i, has an evaluative concern with respect to a topic of concern, then [and only then—but this part will come later] he cannot but have a directive concern with respect to the same topic of concern if he does not want to do something odd or bizarre. This oddity, which may be thought of as a pragmatic fallacy, resembles the so-called "Moore's paradox" in doxastic logic when one says, "Bertrand Russell is a philosopher, but I do not believe it."

Indeed the relationship we tried to characterize above and the oddity we just mentioned can be examined from a different angle. Instead of talking about a person acting as the mouthpiece of a theory of value in making evaluations and issuing commands, we may simply speak of the theory itself. We may think of a theory (of value) as capable of making value judgments and capable of issuing commands. Now, since ethics is commonly taken to be not only a theoretical "science" but also a practical discipline, an ethical doctrine is devised not merely to differentiate the good from the bad, or the right from the wrong, but also to tell people what they ought to do, or what they should try their best to do. Hence, there is no wonder that when a theory (of value) evaluates to a person that a certain state of affairs is good, the theory also issues to him a command that he does his best to bring about that state of affairs. To claim that a theory evaluates a state of affairs as good but also claim that the theory decline to order, or refrains from commanding, the bringing-about of that state of affairs seems to betray a rather odd conception of a value theory, because this conception, among other things, would deprive a value theory of any practical significance and working relevance as a guide of life.

We have, in the above paragraphs, tried to establish a relationship between the evaluative concern (with respect to a topic of concern) and the directive concern (with respect to the same topic of concern) which a person has when he utters sentences in a moral context. We shall now give this relationship a name. We shall say that in a moral context, with respect to a proposition (state of affairs) the evaluative concern *pragmatically entails* the directive concern, meaning that to admit the existence of the evaluative concern and at the same time deny the existence of the directive concern is to run into the inconsistency we described above. Now, since the evaluative concern with respect to a proposition and the directive concern with respect to the same proposition are characteristically *expressed* (in the sense in which Leonard uses the word) by two different sentences *indicating* (again in Leonard's sense) that proposition, we shall extend the use of 'pragmatic entailment' and say that the sentence expressing the evaluative concern pragmatically entails the sentence expressing the directive concern. For example, we shall say that the sentence

(23.14)   It is good for you to be friendly.

pragmatically entails the sentence

(23.15)   Do your best to be friendly!

This, however, is only half of the story. We shall also maintain the converse. That is, that (23.15) also pragmatically entails (23.14) in a moral context. A similar argument applies.

First, consider a theory of value T_i which stipulates, among other things, what is good and/or what is bad. Can it be the case that T_i commands a certain person to do his best to bring about a certain proposition, yet does not claim that it evaluates that proposition as good? The answer seems definitely in the negative. To put the matter in a different way, there would be the same kind of oddity that we noted above if T_i command someone to do his best to do something but does not evaluate that something as good. This seems to be an intolerable oddity. Consequently, a man speaking as the mouthpiece of a value theory, will certainly have the evaluative concern unless he does not have the corresponding directive concern. For instance, when x orders y to be friendly, and y asks for a reason, x shall have the ready answer: "Because it is good". The answer is *ready* not in the sense that x can immediately speak it out, but rather in the sense that when x issues the command, he already "implies" that it is good. If x commands y to do his best to bring it about that p, but declares that p is not good, x either makes a mistake or fails to be a "faithful" mouthpiece of the value theory in question. Indeed, when we say, for example, that honesty is a good policy (evaluation), we want our auditors to be honest (direction); likewise, when we advise or tell someone to be patriotic (direction), we "imply" that patriotism is a good thing (evaluation).

Hence, we shall say that in a moral context the directive concern also pragmatically entails the corresponding evaluative concern. Again, we shall apply the notion of pragmatical entailment to sentences. We shall say, for example, (23.15) pragmatically entails (23.14).

Let us say that two sentences are *pragmatically mutually entailing* or *pragmatically equivalent* if the first pragmatically entails, and is pragmatically entailed by, the second sentence. Let us also say that two concerns with respect to a certain topic of concern are pragmatically mutually entailing or equivalent if they pragmatically entail each other.

Due to this pragmatically mutually entailing relation between the evaluative concern and the directive concern in a moral context, a sentence which characteristically expresses the evaluative concern becomes functionally equivalent with a sentence which characteristically expresses the directive concern, because each sentence pragmatically entails the other. They both have the same dual functions, namely, evaluation and direction. For example, due to this pragmatical relationship between evaluative concern and directive concern, (23.14) and (23.15) can be used *both* to evaluate and at the same time to direct action. Of course, this is not to deny that (23.14) and (23.15) may have different characteristic functions, one of them emphasizes the evaluative side, the other has a stronger directive ring to it.

In order not to go into the different aspects of emphasis of the above-discussed two types of sentences in a value theory, we propose that we use

It is desirable[i] that p

to perform the two functions, evaluation and direction, which are, respectively, the characteristic functions of

It is good[i] that p

and

> Do your best to bring it about that p![i]

The relation between deontic logic and imperative logic will be justified on the same ground.. That is, we shall provide a pragmatical justification.

As we mentioned above, the following expression is to be treated as a basic moral sentence in a theory of duty:

(23.5)   It is required[i] that p^*.

or

(23.6) $R_i p^*$

In the same manner as we maintained above in the case of a theory of value, we shall say that (23.5) is uttered in order to accomplish what the following two sentences will jointly accomplish:

(23.16)   It is obligatory[i] that p^*

or

(23.17) $O_{R_i} p^*$

together with

(23.18)   Bring it about that p^*![i]

which we want to symbolize as

(23.19) $(!_{R_i})\, p^*$

Again, the concern of uttering (23.16) is an evaluative one, and the topic of concern is p^*. On the other hand, the concern of uttering (23.18) is a directive one, but again, the topic of concern is the same p^*. Moreover, just as in the case of a theory of value, these two concerns, evaluation and direction, are pragmatically mutually entailing. Consequently, (23.17) and (23.19) are pragmatically equivalent.

One example: when we say that it is obligatory[i] for someone to help his neighbors (at a certain time in a certain place), we also want him to help his neighbors (at that time in that place.) The reverse is also true. These two concerns are pragmatically mutually entailing as we have repeatedly said. It would be extremely odd for us to proclaim, for example, that it is everyone's duty[i] to be patriotic but to feel completely all right when we see someone act as a traitor. By the same token, it seems that we would be committing nothing short of the aforementioned pragmatic fallacy should we morally command someone to go to fight in Vietnam but at the same time announce that it is not his duty (obligation) to do so.

At this point we shall again stress the fact that when a person makes a (moral) evaluation or issues a (moral) command, he works as if he were the mouthpiece of a set of (moral) rules. It is only under this assumption that we claim his evaluative concern pragmatically entails, and is pragmatically entailed by, his corresponding directive concern. And consequently, a sentence like (23.17) is pragmatically equivalent to another sentence like (23.18). We shall hereafter call sentences of the former type *deontic sentences* and sentence of the latter type *imperative sentences*. What we have so far tried to establish, then, is that a deontic sentence is pragmatically equivalent to the corresponding imperative sentence. They have the same functions or uses, namely, evaluation and direction. Of course, we do not deny that a deontic sentence has evaluation as its characteristic function, and an imperative sentence, on the other hand, has direction as its characteristic function. Hence, a man when making a choice between these two sorts of sentences may have this or that kind of emphasis in mind.

It is on the ground of pragmatic equivalence that we

try to maintain that a system of deontic logic and the corresponding system of imperative logic are but isomorphic models of the same normative logic.

§ 24. NORMATIVE SENTENCES: DEONTIC AND IMPERATIVE

Let us now specify what we mean by a deontic sentence and an imperative sentence which we have already mentioned but have only roughly exemplified and ambiguously identified in the last section. Let us say that an expression is a *deontic formula* (or a deontic sentence form) if and only if it can be formed by a finite application of the following rules:

i) If A* is a CM-act-formula, then ⌜O_RA*⌝ is a (CM-) deontic formula.

ii) If B and C are (CM-) deontic formulas, so are ⌜~ B⌝, ⌜[B & C]⌝, ⌜[B v C]⌝, ⌜[B ⊃ C]⌝ and ⌜[B ≡ C]⌝.

where a CM-act-formula and 'O_R' are understood as they were characterized in the last chapter. As we call 'O_R' a deontic operator, we may analogously call ' ($!_R$) ' an imperative operator. We then proceed to define an *imperative formula* (or an imperative sentence form) as an expression which is formed by a finite application of the following rules:

iii) If A* is a CM-act-formula, then ⌜($!_R$) A*⌝ is a (CM-) imperative formula.

iv) If B and C are (CM-) imperative formulas, so are ⌜~B⌝, ⌜[B & C]⌝, ⌜[B v C]⌝, ⌜[B ⊃ C]⌝ and ⌜[B ≡ C]⌝.

It may be noted that in imperative logic, it is of special interest to write an imperative formula in the following special form:

(24.1) $(\text{You}, \beta, \gamma)\, A$

in which 'you' denotes as usual the person (s) addressed, and 'β' and 'γ' are variables, as specified in § 19, for time and location, respectively. And, finally, 'A' denotes an act.

For instance, the following addressed to John

(24.2)   (You, this coming Friday, Rm. 14, Morrill Hall)
          coming - to - take - the - final - examination.

may be rendered in everyday English as the following sentence:

(24.3)   John, come to take the final examination this
          coming Friday in room 14, Morrill Hall!

After we have defined a deontic formula and an imperative formula, the definition of a deontic sentence and that of an imperative sentence become straightforward. We may simply say that a sentence is deontic (imperative) if it instantiates a deontic (imperative) formula. And a sentence is *normative* if it is either deontic or imperative.

For example, (24.4) below is a deontic sentence.

(24.4)   It is obligatory[i] for John to go to help his
          neighbors in their houses when they need him.

Because it instantiates the following deontic formula:

$$O_{R_i}\,(\alpha, \beta, \gamma)\, A$$

or, in short,

$$O_R p^*$$

(24.5) below, on the other hand, is an imperative sentence.

(24.5)   You, close the door right now, and go to tell
          John it is raining![i]

which exhibits the following imperative formula:

(24.6) $(!_{R_i})\, [\,(\text{you}, \beta, \gamma)\, A_1 \,\&\, (\text{you}, \beta', \gamma')\, A_2]$

Of course, to identify a particular deontic or imperative

sentence often requires insight. Sometimes paraphrasing is needed before we can tell whether or not a sentence is deontic or imperative or something else.

Since it is sometimes desirable to make the agent, time, and location constant as in the case of deontic logic, we shall, again, in imperative logic, use 'p*' to abbreviate a CM-act-formula. We shall thus write (24.6) as, e. g.,

(24.7) $(!_{R_i})$ $(p^* \& q^*)$

The difference between the expression abbreviated by 'p*' and that in which 'you' appears is that in the latter the variable for agents *always* takes as its substituent expression the second person pronoun, namely, 'you'. But when we render an imperative sentence into every day language, the 'you', as appeared in (24.5), is as a rule omitted. We simply say 'Close the door!' instead of 'You, close the door!' except for emphasis.

On several earlier occasions we noted that there are other forms of deontic formulas which can be defined in terms of $\ulcorner O_R A^* \urcorner$ together with sentential connectives, particularly, '~' and '&'. For instance, the following definitions show that at least three other forms of deontic formulas are available, namely, $\ulcorner P_R A^* \urcorner$, $\ulcorner F_R A^* \urcorner$ and $\ulcorner I_R A^* \urcorner$.

(D17.2) $\ulcorner P_R A^* \urcorner =_{Df} \ulcorner \sim O_R \sim A^* \urcorner$

(D17.3) $\ulcorner F_R A^* \urcorner =_{Df} \ulcorner \sim P_R A^* \urcorner$

(D17.4) $\ulcorner I_R A^* \urcorner =_{Df} \ulcorner P_R A^* \& P_R \sim A^* \urcorner$

where 'A*' is any CM-act-formula, say, 'p*'

Now, in a close analogy, we may try to set up in imperative logic the following definitions corresponding to the above ones, to characterize three other forms of imperative formulas. These definitions are:

(D24.1) $\quad \ulcorner (\sqrt{}_R) A^* \urcorner =_{Df} \ulcorner \sim (!_R) \sim A^* \urcorner$

(D24.2) $\quad \ulcorner (X_R) A^* \urcorner =_{Df} \ulcorner \sim (\sqrt{}_R) A^* \urcorner$

(D24.3) $\quad \ulcorner (\#_R) A^* \urcorner =_{Df} \ulcorner (\sqrt{}_R) A^* \& (\sqrt{}_R) \sim A^* \urcorner$

A note is immediately needed here to explain how to read the definitions (D24.1) — (D24.3). We shall, in particular, explain how it is meaningful to prefix a tilde to an imperative sentence like $\ulcorner \sim (!_R) \sim A^* \urcorner$ in the *definiens* of (D24.1). First, we may think of an imperative sentence.

(24.8) $\qquad$ Bring it about that A^*!

or

(24.9) $\qquad (!_R) A^*$

as true (where A^* is a CM-act-proposition), if and only if a certain mouthpiece, say x, of moral rules R commands that A^* be brought about. Hence, the negation of (24.8) or (24.9) is true if and only if x does *not* command that A be brought about. According to this rendering, (D24.1) can be read as: "$(\sqrt{}_R) A^*$ is commanded by x if and only if, by definition, $(!_R) \sim A^*$ is not commanded by x." But x is nothing more than the mouthpiece of R, hence, we may have a more straightforward way to read (D24.1) — (D24.3). We may simply read (D24.1) as rules R makes the command $(\sqrt{}) A^*$ if and only if R does not require that $\sim A^*$ be brought about. (D24.2) and (D24.3) can be similarly understood.

Just as 'P_R', 'F_R', and 'I_R' may also be thought of as deontic operators, '$(\sqrt{}_R)$', '(X_R)', and '$(\#_R)$' may be regarded as three new imperative operators in addition to the usual imperative operator '$(!_R)$'.

Of these three new imperative operators, '(X_R)' is hardly new to our intuition, it answers quite closely to our everyday notion of "Do not...!" in "Do not bring it about that p*!" In contrast with our intuitive familiarity of '(X_R)', we find no counterparts for '$(\sqrt{}_R)$' and '$(\#_R)$' in English. However, non-existence in our natural language is not in the least a disproof of the possibility, or even plausibility, of these imperative operators. The lack or unconvention- ality of these two imperative operators must be considered, from a logical point of view, as purely accidental, although the phenomenon is psychologically and practically explainable.

In our daily life, when we come near to using the imperative notions corresponding to '$(\sqrt{}_R)$' and '$(\#_R)$', we simply use their deontic counterparts 'P_R' and 'I_R', namely, 'You may...' or 'It is permissible that you...' and "It is indifferent that you...". This is another place to appreciate the pragmatic relationship between deontic operators and imperative operators, and, in general, between deontic logic and imperative logic.

§ 25. THREE CORRESPONDING SYSTEMS OF IMPERATIVE LOGIC: CMI_RT^*, CMI_RS4^* AND CMI_RS5^*

Our conviction that a deontic logic and its corresponding imperative logic are but two models of a certain normative theory finds a justification in what we have said above concerning the close relation between evaluation and direction in the moral use of language. This conviction immediately gives rise to the following result: to each system of deontic logic we have specified in § 19, namely, CMO_RT^*, CMO_RS4^* and CMO_RS5^*, there corresponds a system of imperative logic closely related to it. Let us call the imperative systems corresponding to the above-mentioned deontic systems CMI_RT^*, CMI_RS4^* and CMI_RS5^*, respectively. The prefix 'CM', again, reminds us that imperative operators take CM-act-formulas as their operands.

These three systems of imperative logic may now be outlined as follows:

I. Vocabulary (for all three systems alike):
Same as the vocabulary of CMO_RT^* in § 19 except that iii) now reads:
vii) Imperative operator: ' $(!_R)$ '

II. Formation rules (again, for each of those three systems):
Same as that of CMO_RT^* except that each occurrence of 'deontic term' in the rules is now replaced by an occurrence of 'imperative term'. Furthermore, vii) is

cancelled in favor of the following:

vii')   If A is a wff, so is $\ulcorner \sim (!_R) A \urcorner$.

We may, as shown in the last section, introduce other imperative operators by means of the definitions (D24.1) — (D24.3).

III. Theoremhood (including axiomhood) :

We shall say that

$$\mathbf{S}.^{\text{'}O_R\text{'}}_{\text{'}!_R\text{'}} \text{ (THM)} \bigg|$$

is a theorem of $CMI_R T^*$ (or $CMI_R S4^*$, or $CMI_R S5^*$) provided that (THM) is a theorem of $CMO_R T^*$ (or $CMO_R S4^*$, or $CMO_R S5^*$).

Let us agree to use the same numbering for the theorems of $CMI_R T^* — CMI_R S5^*$ as for the theorems of $CMO_R T^* — CMO_R S5^*$ except that we prefix '$CMI_R T^*$' and so on rather than '$CMO_R T^*$' and so forth, to the numerals.

For example, the following is a theorem of $CMI_R T^*$

$(CMI_R T^* 19)$ $\sim [(!_R) p^* \& (!_R) \sim p^*]$

which is also $(CMI_R S4^* 19)$ and $(CMI_R S5^* 19)$.

As we recall, systems $CMO_R T^* — CMO_R S5^*$ of deontic logic are designed only to formalize a certain unspecified partial notion of obligation. Thus, we defined in § 17 '$O_R A^*$' as "R requires that A^*". In the same manner, systems $CMI_R T^* — CMI_R S5^*$ of imperative logic are meant only to systematize a certain unspecified partial notion of "do!", or "Bring it about that...!" That is to say, a certain mouth-piece or, if we like, a certain authority, of a certain set of moral rules is always assumed as standing behind this partial imperative notion. If we let 'AR' stand for a certain mouthpiece of the set of moral rules R, or a certain moral authority created to enforce the set of moral rules R, we may try to characterize the partial imperative notion of "Do!" by the following definition.

(D25.1) $\ulcorner (!_R) A^* \urcorner =_{Df}$ AR commands that A^* be brought about.

We use 'A^*' instead of 'A' to emphasize that the operand of '$(!_R)$' is a CM-act-formula.

But a moral authority or mouthpiece can either be identified with, or else be thought of as, nothing but an instrument or an agent created, as we said above, to enforce a set of moral rules. That is, a moral authority must satisfy the following condition:

(25.2) AR commands that A^* be brought about if and only if R requires that A^*

Hence, instead of (D25.1) we may set up the following definition.

(D25.3) $\ulcorner (!_R) A^* \urcorner =_{Df}$ R requires that A^*

Compare (D25.3) with (D17.1), i.e., with

(D17.1) $\ulcorner O_R A^* \urcorner =_{Df}$ R requires that A^*

It may, at first sight, seem very strange that an imperative operator and a deontic operator are defined in exactly the same terms. That is, by means of the requirement of R. A closer examination, however, will remove any misgivings. First, as we have repeatedly stressed, the two functions of language in a moral context are pragmatically equivalent. Thus, we have said in § 23 that when we utter

(23.5) It is required[i] that p^*

or

(25.4) R_i requires that p^*

we want to accomplish what the following two utterances

may jointly accomplish:

(23.12) $O_R p^*$

and

(23.14) $(!_R) p^*$

That is to say, on the deontic side, (25.4) "means" the same as (23.12) but on the imperative side, it has the "same meaning" as (23.14).

We have then explained '$(!_R)$' in terms of the requirement of a particular set of moral rules R. Consequently, what we have said in § 18 applies, without further ado, to the case of imperative logic. In particular, we shall remind ourselves of the following: that a set of moral rules is always consistent, hence $(CMI_R T^*19)$ above is always true. But the union set of all the sets of rules may not be consistent; it may be absolutely inconsistent or practically inconsistent. Furthermore, because a person may submit himself to incompatible orders, the imperative version of conflicting duties, i.e., conflicting orders, is possible.

As in the case of CM-deontic systems, it is easy to see that quantifiers are readily introducible into CM-imperative systems. For example, the following saying of Confucius can be satisfactorily formulated only in quantified imperative logic.

(25.5)   Do not do to others what you do not want others to do to you!

Even such a simple command as

(25.6)   Keep your promises!

demands the use of quantifiers to be symbolized adequately. Hence, it seems beyond question that quantifiers are indispensable in an imperative logic comprehensive enough to cope with our ordinary imperative arguments. The reason for this indispensability can be further appreciated if we recall our remarks in § 22 on the indispensability of quantifiers in deontic logic.

Let us, again, call an imperative system a *first-order imperative logic,* if we allow the quantifiers to bind only individual variables. When a system admits of quantifiers which bind imperative operators, it will be called a *second-order imperative* logic. A closer investigation of quantified imperative logic is beyond the scope of our present discussion.

The difficulties and "paradoxes" which puzzle people in the so-called "old" systems of deontic logic can be reformulated in a revised form in imperative logic. Moreover, our proposed solutions apply equally well in imperative logic.

§ 26. PURE NORMATIVE LOGICS: THE LOGICS OF REQUIREMENT CMRT*, CMRS4* AND CMRS5*

Having observed that an imperative system can be constructed as an isomorphic model of a corresponding deontic system, and that these two different logics have common bases in pragmatics and the formal theory of ethics, we might naturally expect, as we anticipated earlier, there to be a *pure normative logic* of which a deontic system and its corresponding imperative system are nothing but two specific models. The primitive notion of this pure normative logic is

(26.1)   R requires that...

or, in symbols

(26.2)   R

Hence, the resulting system may be called the *logic of requirement*. But again, we formalize only a partial notion of requirement.

It suffices to mention that we are able to easily construct three systems of pure normative logic CMRT*, CMRS4* and CMRS5* of which CMO_RT, CMO_RS4* and CMO_RS5* on the one hand, and CMI_RT*, CMI_RS4* and CMI_RS5* on the other hand are, respectively, deontic and imperative models. After we have seen the primitive bases of CMO_RT*, etc., it is trivial to set down the primitive bases for CMRT* —CMRS5*. We shall also use the same numbering to list the theorems. For example, the following is a theorem of CMRT*:

(CMRT*19) $\sim[Rp^* \& R \sim p^*]$

of which the following is its deontic counterpart:

(CMO$_R$T*19) $\sim[O_R p^* \& O_R \sim p^*]$

and the following, its imperative one:

(CMI$_R$T*19) $\sim[\,(!_R)\,p^* \& (!_R) \sim p^*]$

The assumptions and consequences of meta-ethics in §18 are now directly related to the concept of requirement which the pure normative logic is set up to formalize.

Again, quantifiers can be introduced. And we may talk about *first-order* and *second-order* pure normative logic.

Consequently, we may want to put more attention directly to pure normative logic, or the logic of require-ment. However, since the names 'deontic logic' and, especially, 'imperative logic' have long been well established in the literature, and since the expressions which are usually incorporated in these logics are far more conventional than the expressions we might find in the logic of requirement, we shall continue to talk about deontic logic and imperative logic. But we understand that what we have already said and shall have said about these logics can be readily mapped onto the logic of requirement. [1]

---

[1] In a similar manner, we might construct a *pure logic of value* (which formalizes the concept of desirability) of which the logic of goodness (which formalizes the concept of goodness) and the logic of moral injunction (which formalizes the concept of "Do your best to bring it about that...!) are two specific models.

§ 27. NORMATIVE ARGUMENTS: PURE AND MIXED

An argument, as usual, is understood as a sequence B_1, B_2, B_3,...B_k, C of sentences, the last sentence C is called the *conclusion*, the other sentences B_1, B_2, B_3, ..., B_k are called the *premisses* A premiss is a premiss *of* an argument, and a conclusion is a conclusion *of* an argument.

We shall say that an argument is *assertoric* if its conclusion is an assertoric sentence; [1] it is *deontic* if its conclusion is a deontic sentence; and it is *imperative* if its conclusion is an imperative sentence. Deontic arguments and imperative arguments are said to be *normative* arguments.

If all the premisses and the conclusion of an argument are made up of the same type of sentences, the argument is said to be *pure,* that is, either a pure assertoric argument or a pure deontic argument or a pure imperative argument. Otherwise, it is *mixed*. When an argument is a normative one, it will be called a *uniform* argument provided that its normative premisses are of the same type of sentence as its conclusion. It will be said to be *non-uniform,* if otherwise. A uniform (normative) argument is

---

[1] By an assertoric sentence we mean either a factual or empirical sentence like "Paris is the capital of the United States" (which *is* false) or a logical or analytical sentence like "A black raven is black" (which is *necessarily* true.)

either a uniform deontic argument or a uniform imperative argument.

For example, the following are all pure.

(27.1)   John keeps all his promises.
         This is his promise.
         ∴ John keeps it.

(27.2)   John ought^i to keep his promises.
         John ought^i to help his neighbors.
         ∴ John ought^i to keep his promises and help his neighbors.

(27.3)   Be honest!^{i}
         ∴ Do not cheat!^{i}

where (27.1) is a pure assertoric argument; (27.2), a pure deontic argument; and (27.3), a pure imperative argument.

On the other hand, the following arguments are mixed ones:

(27.4)   All and only logicians ought^i to teach logic.
         John is a logician.
         ∴ John is permitted^i to teach logic.

(27.5)   It is your duty^i to help John.
         ∴ Help John!^{i}

(27.6)   Only senior members are permitted^i to speak at the club meeting.
         John speaks at the club meeting.
         ∴ John is a senior member.

(27.7)   Help your neighbors and only your neighbors!^{i}
         Help John!^{i}
         ∴ John is your neighbor.

(27.4) is a mixed deontic argument, (27.5), a mixed imperative one. Both are mixed normative arguments. On the other hand, (27.6) and (27.7) are mixed assertoric arguments. Among the normative arguments we have listed above, i.e., (27.2), (27.3), (27.4) and (27.5), two are uniform, namely (27.2) and (27.3), while (27.4) and (27.5) are not. (We regard (27.4) as uniform, because there is only one sort of normative sentence involved in the whole argument.)

An immediate remark is in order. In our discussion, a normative sentence is one in which the normative operator —a deontic operator or an imperative operator—take CM-act-sentences and only CM-act-sentences as its operands. In the above examples, we have, however, for the sake of brevity and naturalness, made use of normative sentences that are at most incomplete forms of certain full-fledged normative sentences. We acted nevertheless on the tacit assumption that the resumption to full-fledged normative sentences is always possible. We shall in the same manner, restrict our attention, for the time being, to assertoric sentences of a special type, namely, CM-act-sentences. Again, we assume that every assertoric sentence we used or shall use can be translated into a full-fledged CM-act-sentence.

Up to this point, we have exhibited arguments of a relatively simple type. The simplicity lies in the fact that each premiss and conclusion of each argument we dealt with is either an assertoric sentence, a deontic sentence, or an imperative sentence, exclusively. We did not examine, for example, arguments such as the one below:

(27.8)   If one ever feels sad, read Psalm 23![i]

John is sad.

∴ John ought[i] to read Psalm 23.

in which there are some component sentences which are

further made up of different types of sentences. In the case of (27.8) the first premiss is conditional sentence having an assertoric sentence as its antecedent and an imperative sentence as its consequent. We may call a sentence of this type a *multi-natured* or a *multiplex* sentence. In general, '$\Theta^k(A_1, A_2, ... A_k)$' is a k-place multiplex sentence if 'Θ^k' is a k-place sentential connective and there exist i and j (i, j = 1, 2, ..., k) such that $i \neq j$ and A_i and A_j are of different sentence type. That is, '$\Theta^k(A_1, A_2, ..., A_k)$' is a k-place multiplex sentence, if in the list $A_1, A_2, ... A_k$ of sentence, at least two are not of the same type. More specifically, we shall say that a sentence is *assertoric-deontic* (or deontic-assertoric) if it is composed of assertoric sentences and deontic sentences. Analogously, we may have an *assertoric-imperative* sentence, a *deontic-imperative* sentence, an *assertoric-imperative-deontic* sentence, and so on.

In what follows, we shall confine ourselves mainly to the discussion of normative arguments, uniform or non-uniform, multiplex or otherwise, together with assertoric arguments with normative premisses. Pure assertoric arguments will be treated merely in passing.

§ 28. TOWARD A DEFINITION
OF NORMATIVE VALIDITY

When we talk about arguments, one of the most important problems is the problem of validity. Roughly speaking, an argument

(28.1) $A_1, A_2, A_3, ..., A_k,$ $\therefore$ C

is said to be *valid* if and only if its conclusion 'C' *follows logically* from its premisses

(28.2) $A_1, A_2, A_3, ..., A_k$

Or, we may say, in other words, that (28.1) is valid if and only if (28.2) *logically entails* 'C'. The problem, however, is how to characterize the relation of "logical following" or "logical entailing" holding between the premisses and the conclusion of an argument.

But before we go to the very core of the discussion of validity of normative arguments, certain remarks and preliminary explanations are necessary. They will facilitate our later presentation and prevent misunderstanding.

First of all, it may be recalled that we have, upon the basis of the close relation that exists between a deontic sentence and its corresponding imperative sentence, defined a deontic sentence and its imperative counterpart in terms of the same *definiens*. In particular, '$O_R p^*$' and '$(!_R) p^*$' are both defined as 'R requires that p*'. Moreover, we have indicated in § 24 that the truth condition of '$(!_R) p^*$' can also be specified in terms of the requirement of R. We said that '$(!_R) p^*$' is true if and only if R requires that p*.

The same remarks are applicable to '$O_R p^*$'. We may, for instance, say—and this will be explicitly put down later— that '$O_R p^*$' is true, again, if and only if R requires that p^*.

It is then clear that, according to our construing, a deontic sentence and its corresponding imperative sentence both have the same truth conditions. It follows that they are mutually replaceable *salve veritate* in any formula in an extensional context. In addition, since we shall try to define the validity of a normative argument in terms of truth, those two sentences are also inferentially interchangeable *salve validitate*. Consequently, the validity of a deontic argument and the validity of an imperative argument are judged on the same footing. They have, so to speak, the same "logic". For instance, what can be used to justify the following imperative argument

(28.3)   If one ever feels sad, one ought[i] to read Psalm 23.

John is sad.

∴ John, read Psalm 23![i]

will be regarded as equally appropriately employed to justify the following deontic one:

(27.8)   If one ever feels sad, read Psalm 23![i]

John is sad.

∴ John ought[i] to read Psalm 23.

They will be regarded, syntactically or inferentially, as the same argument.

Secondly, in classical (assertoric) logic, we have, more often than not, used the concept of truth to explicate the concept of validity. For instance, we frequently characterize a valid argument as one of which the conclusion cannot but be true provided that all the premises are true. Now, this definition is transferrable, with little substantial further ado, to the case of normative arguments, since, as indicated above, we regard a deontic sentence and an imperative sentence as being true or false, [1] and, as we shall see later, the usual definition of validity provides us with a very plausible criterion of "good" or "correct" normative arguments.

A final remark is now in order. It may be argued that, in one sense, the definition of validity *within* our normative systems outlined in earlier sections is trivial, or, at least, straightforward. We may simply say, for example, that a normative argument.

(28.1) $A_1, A_2, A_3, ..., A_k, \quad \therefore C$

is valid if and only if

(28.9) $A_1 \& A_2 \& A_3 \& ... \& A_k \supset C$

is an instance of a theorem of our system. [2] Thus, we may differentiate between CMRT*-*validity*. CMRS4*-*validity* and CMRS5*-*validity* [3]. Of course, it goes without saying that the first sense of validity entails the second one; and the second, the third.

However, what we try to accomplish in this section

---

1 Henry S. Leonard is among those philosophers who would say that normative sentences are on an equal footing as assertoric sentences insofar as their truth values are concerned. See Leonard [1959a] and [1961]. For a criticism of Leonard's position, see, e.g. Wheatley, J.M.O., "Note on Professor Leonard's Analysis of Interrogatives, etc.", *Philosophy of Science*, vol. 28, pp. 52-54, 1961; and Stahl, G., Review of Leonard [1959a], [1961], etc., *Journal of Symbolic Logic*, vol. 31, pp. 666-668, 1966.

2 'C', in this case, is a normative sentence, of course.

3 Just as we have OT* validity, OS4* validity and OS5* validity in § 20.

and the following ones is something quite different. We want to outline a theory which may be called the *intuitive theory of normative validity*, or perhaps more adequately, the *general theory of normative validity*. Roughly speaking, such a theory is a stipulation of a criterion or a definition which distinguish the correct normative arguments from others which are not correct. Such a general theory of validity is of special interest because of the fact that, up to the present, there is no normative logic which is universally accepted and may be called *the* logic of normative arguments. Our theory may be thought of as a preliminary explication of our intuitive concept of normative validity.

But before we attempt such a definition or criterion of validity for a normative argument, let us talk a little about our motivation in setting down such a definition. First, let us say that a normative sentence is used to make evaluations and/or to issue commands, just as an assertoric sentence is typically used to describe states of affairs or to give information. Now, a good or correct (pure) assertoric argument can be intuitively conceived as one of which the conclusion describes states of affairs that are already described or contained in the premises. Or, we may say that a correct assertoric argument is one of which the conclusion gives information that is already given in the premises. For example, if we assert:

(28.12)   John and Mary have blue eyes.

we may infer that

(28.13)   John has blue eyes.

for the information given in (28.13) is already contained in the information given in (28.12). Thus, the argument of which (28.12) is the premiss and (28.13) the conclusion is a correct or good argument. On the other hand, when one asserts

(28.14)   I feel pain when I kick what I believe to be a stone.

one cannot correctly infer, as Samuel Johnson seemed to want to infer, that

(28.15)   A stone exists.

Indeed, one cannot even correctly infer, as Bertrand Russell points out, that

(28.16)   My foot exists.

That is, the reasoning from (28.14) to (28.15) or from (28.14) to (28.16) is not a good argument. The information given in (28.15) or in (28.16) is not already contained in (28.14).

Here we may think of making a logical reasoning as an effort to bring up some information which is contained in the information already given in the first place. Logical reasoning can never provide us with genuinely new information. Thus, we find Carl G. Hempel saying that logical reasoning may make explicit what is already contained implicitly in the premises, but it cannot yield something which is really new (Hempel calls it *theoretically new*).[4]

In a close analogy, we may think of a (pure) normative argument as one by means of which people want to reason from certain evaluations and/or commands to certain (other) evaluations and/or commands. If the evaluations made, or the commands issued, in the conclusion of a (normative)

4 See Hempel, "On the Nature of Mathematical Truth", reprinted in P. Benacerraf and H. Putnam (ed.), *Philosophy of Mathematics*, p. 379.

argument are already contained, perhaps implicitly, in the evaluations or commands made or issued in the premisses, then we say that this argument is good or correct. Otherwise, it is not a correct argument. For example, the evaluation made in

(28.17)   It is obligatory for John to help his neighbors.

is contained in the evaluation made in

(28.18)   It is obligatory for John to help his neighbors and keep all his promises.

Hence, the (deontic) argument which consists of (28.18) as its premiss and (28.17) as its conclusion is a correct one. Likewise, the command which is issued in

(28.19)   Do not do to others what you do not want other to do to you!

is contained in the command issued in

(28.20)   Do not do to others what you do not want others to do to you, [but] do unto others as you would that they do unto you!

Hence, the (imperative) argument from (28.20) to (28.19) is a good one.

On the contrary, the argument from (28.17) to (28.18) or the argument from (28.19) to (28.20) is not a good argument, because in each case the conclusion makes an evaluation (or issues a command) which is not already contained in the premiss.

The utility of distinguishing the good normative arguments from those that are bad can also be better appreciated if we first make a comparison by looking into the usefulness of distinguishing good assertoric arguments from others which are not. Let

(28.1) $A_1, A_2, A_3, ..., A_k, \quad \therefore \quad C$

as specified before be a (pure) assertoric argument, and
suppose that it is a good one. Since it is good, the information contained in 'C' is already contained in the conjunction of

(28.2) $A_1, A_2, A_3, ..., A_k$

Now, let us think of a piece of information as either true
or false *in* a world W, since (28.1) is a good argument,
we know that 'C' conveys true information in a world W
provided that what (28.2) jointly conveys is true information in W. This follows from the fact that the information
conveyed in 'C' is contained in the information conveyed
jointly in (28.2). Thus, we see that by recognizing that a
certain argument, say (28.1) is a good argument, we know
that a certain piece of information, say that which is conveyed in 'C', can be "extracted" from another piece (or
other pieces) of information, for instance, that (those) which
is (are) conveyed jointly in (28.2). This seems to answer
cogently to our intellectual curiosity and practical utility,
too, of finding out whether a piece of information *logically*
follows from another piece (or other pieces) of information when we use such a locution as 'from ..., it follows
(logically) that ...'.

    To be more precise, instead of talking about a piece
of information or pieces of information, let us speak of a
proposition or propositions understanding tacitly that the
piece of information conveyed in a sentence—we know
that what are the premises and conclusion of an argument
are certain sentences—is the proposition denoted or indicated
by that sentence. After this transference, it is easily seen
that by recognizing a certain argument as a good one, we
know that a certain proposition, i.e., the one which is

indicated by the conclusion of this argument, can be "extracted" from another proposition or other propositions, i.e., one (s) indicated by the premiss (es). Now, a proposition is thought of as true or false *in* a world W, and sentence is true or false in W if and only if the proposition it indicates is true or false in W. Thus, the relation of "logical following", now to be defined on the set of sentences, can be reconstructed, as we commonly see, in the following way:

(C28.21)   'C' logically follows from (28.2) if and only if, in every world W, 'C' would be true in W if 'A_1', 'A_2', 'A_3', ..., 'A_k' should all be true in W.

We shall say that (28.2) *logically entails* 'C' if and only if 'C' logically follows from (28.2). Now, a good or correct argument can be identified as one of which the premisses logically entail the conclusion. A good argument is also called a *valid* argument.

Let us now turn our attention to the case of normative arguments. The utility of a definition or criterion of normative validity can be understood in a similar way as we understand the usefulness of a criterion of validity for assertoric arguments. Just as by recognizing a valid assertoric argument, we are able to "extract" some proposition from other propositions because of their "containing" relation, by recognizing a normative argument as being good or valid, we should be, or want to be, able to extract some evaluation from other evaluations and/or some command from other commands. Or, in other words, if we should know that a (normative) argument is good, then we would be able to tell that the evaluation conveyed by the conclusion is made (by a certain set of rules), provided that the evaluations conveyed by the premisses (jointly) are made (by that set of rules), or that the command expressed by the conclusion is issued (by a certain set of rules) if the commands expressed by the premisses are issued (by that set of rules). If the relationship we just depicted holds between the premisses and the conclusion of a (pure) normative argument, then we shall say that the argument is *valid*. Or, we shall say that the premisses *logically entail* the conclusion, or that the conclusion *logically follows* from the premisses. To explore a general theory of normative validity may then be thought of as an effort to explicate these logical properties (e. g., validity) and relations (e.g., entailment) in a normative logical context.

The utility of a criterion of normative validity can now be put as follows:

(28.22)   When a (pure) normative argument is known to be valid, then we know that if such and such evaluations—namely, those conveyed in the premisses—are made, then thus and thus an evaluation—namely, that conveyed in the conclusion—*must* also be made; or that if such and such commands are issued, then thus and thus a command *must* also be issued.

Instead of talking separately about evaluations and commands, we shall henceforth use 'prescriptions' to mean 'evaluations and/or commands'. Our (28.22) then reads:

(28.23)   When a (pure) normative argument is known to be valid, then we know that if such and such prescriptions—namely, those expressed in the premisses of the argument—are made, then thus and thus a prescription—namely, that expressed in the conclusion of the argument—*must* also be made.

A remark is immediately called for. When we say above that if such and such prescriptions are made then thus and thus a prescription must also be made, we do not mean that the latter prescription must actually be made by a person or a set of rules. What we mean is that, given that the former prescriptions are made (actually), then *logically* the latter prescription cannot but have already been made, regardless whether the person or the rules explicitly mention the latter prescription or not. To see this point more clearly, we again begin with an example in assertoric logic. Suppose an old man uttered the following sentence just before his death:

(28.24)   All my three sons are blue-eyed.

Suppose further that he had made no other assertions in his life. Then we can say that the man had never *actually* asserted the following:

(28.25)   My eldest son is blue-eyed.

But we shall say that he had *logically* asserted (28.25), because what (28.25) asserts is already contained in the assertion conveyed in (28.24).

Likewise, suppose the old man made the following request—a kind of command, a "soft" one, if we like—before his death:

(28.26)   Give my best wishes to all my three sons!

Suppose again that he had never made any other commands, then he had never actually thus requested:

(28.27)   Give my best wishes to my eldest son!

But since the command issued in (28.27) is already contained in the command issued in (28.26), we shall say

that the old man logically made the command expressed
in (28.27).

§ 29. THE CRITERION OF NORMATIVE VALIDITY

We shall now set out to attend to what we called the general theory of normative validity. To outline the theory, let us begin with simpler forms of arguments. We shall first consider those pure normative arguments of which no component sentences are "molecular", or multiplex, of course. For the reason which should be obvious by now, we shall consider only deontic arguments, leaving imperative arguments aside. By deontic sentences we include O_R-sentences, F_R-sentences and I_R-sentences.

In the first place, we assume, as aforesaid, a consistent set R of moral rules [1] such that for each CM-act-sentence A* the following condition holds:

(29.1) $\qquad O_R A^*$ or $F_R A^*$ or $I_R A^*$

In addition, we shall define the *truth value* of a deontic sentence (*in* a world W) in the following way:

(D29.2)   i) Every deontic sentence D is either true or false in a world W.

         ii) If $D = \ulcorner O_R A^* \urcorner$, then D is true in W if and only if R requires that A* in W.

         iii) If $D = \ulcorner P_R A^* \urcorner$, then D is true in W if and only if R does not require that $\ulcorner \sim A^* \urcorner$ in W.

         iv) If $D = \ulcorner F_R A^* \urcorner$, then D is true in W if and

1 Cf. §§ 17f.

only if R requires that $\ulcorner \sim A^* \urcorner$ in W. [2]

The truth values of truth-functions of deontic sentences can be defined in the usual way, namely,

(D29.3)   v)   D is true in W if and only if $\ulcorner \sim D \urcorner$ is false in W.

     vi) $\ulcorner [D_1 \& D_2] \urcorner$ is true in W if and only if both D_1 and D_2 are true in W.

     vii) $\ulcorner [D_1 \vee D_2] \urcorner$ is true in W if and only if either D_1 is true in W or D_2 is true in W.

     viii) $\ulcorner [D_1 \supset D_2] \urcorner$ is true in W if and only if either D_1 is false in W or D_2 is true in W.

These definitions, i.e., (D29.2) and (D29.3), may be regarded as depicting the truth conditions for deontic sentences of the form $\Phi_R A^*$ and the truth-functions thereof, where Φ_R is a deontic operator and A^*, as we said above, is a CM-act-sentence of any complexity. It may be noted that sentences containing iterated deontic operators will not be discussed and that deontic sentences of the form $\Phi_R A^*$ will not be further broken into their constituent parts.

From these remarks we immediately see that (D29.2) and (D29.3) are not sufficient to characterize the truth value of every deontic sentence. For example, from the truth of

(29.2)   It is obligatory that John goes to school on July 14, 1968 for the committee meeting. $(O_R p^*)$

our definitions do not tell us whether the following sentence is true or not:

---

2 These definitions can be applied to imperative sentences. Simply change 'deontic' to 'imperative', 'O_R' to '$!_R$', and so on, in these definitions.

(29.3)   It is obligatory that John goes to school on July
            14, 1968, for the committee meeting or for the
            final examination. $(O_R (p^* \lor q^*))$

Although our definitions do give the truth value of

(29.4)   It is permitted that John goes fishing with Mark
            or it is permitted that John stays at home study-
            ing logic. [3] $(P_R p_1^* \lor P_R q_1^*)$

based upon the truth value of

(29.5)   It is permitted that John goes fishing with Mark.
            $(P_R p_1^*)$

That means, if we try to develop a system of normative
logic, and (D29.2) — (D29.3) are all the "semantic rules" we
have, then our theory, insofar as its semantics is concerned,
would be limited in the same way that truth-functional
logic is limited in not being applicable to traditional cate-
gorical syllogisms. However, this does not mean that the
definition or criterion of normative validity which we are
going to lay down below must also be impaired in any way.
Just as the usual definition of (assertoric) validity is as
applicable to the traditional theory of syllogism as it is to
propositional logic, our definition of normative validity is
meant to be applicable to normative arguments in general.

    Although our semantic rules laid down above are not
complete as we just said, in many cases our semantics can
be augumented by the results we arrived at in the earlier
sections. For example, if we know '$O_R p^*$' is true, our
semantic rules do not tell us the truth value of '$F_R \sim p^*$, but

---

[3] We shall not write down a full-fledged CM-act-sentence all' the
time, but shall tacitly understand that a resumption to such a
sentence is always possible.

since we have the following as a theorem in our deontic systems:

(CMO$_R$T*2) $O_R p^* \equiv F_R \sim p^*$

we know that '$F_R \sim p^*$' is also true. Similarly, there are other theorems we shall find useful in this respect. However, the use of previous theorems in this manner must be regarded as "extra-systematic", although, as we did say above, some theorems are common to most systems of deontic logic and hence can be used with fairly good confidence. Besides, (16.17) and (16.19) in § 16 turn out to be useful in this respect.

Now our definition of normative validity. The definition we shall propose is actually a direct transplantation of our usual definition of assertoric validity, [4] viz.,

(C29.6)   A pure normative argument

A$_1$, A$_2$, A$_3$,..., A$_k$,   ∴ C

where each 'A$_i$' and 'C' is a deontic sentence, is said to be valid if and only if, in every possible world W, the conclusion 'C' would be true should the premises 'A$_1$', 'A$_2$', 'A$_3$', ..., 'A$_k$' all be true.

To see that this definition or criterion of normative validity explicates the intuitive notion of logical following or entailing, we first recall the definitions (D29.2) which say under what conditions a deontic sentence is said to be true. The criterion (C29.6) then is tantamount to saying that, in every possible world, the rules R would make the prescription expressed in 'C' should the rules make the prescriptions expressed in 'A$_1$', 'A$_2$', 'A$_3$', ..., and 'A$_k$'. This,

---

4 Cf. (C28. 21) in § 28.

in turn, means that, in every possible world, what is expressed by 'C' is a logical consequence of the prescriptions
made by 'A₁', 'A₂', 'A₃', ... and 'A_k'.

For example, the following is a valid deontic argument:

(29.7)   It is obligatory that John goes to fight in
              Vietnam. (O_Rp^*)

         ∴ It is permissible that John goes to fight in
              Vietnam. (P_Rp^*)

This is a valid argument, because it cannot be the case
that 'O_Rp^*' be true but 'P_Rp^*' be false.

We shall, as we indicated before, use 'validity', 'logically
follows' and 'logically entails' in the context of normative
arguments. When a normative argument is valid, we say
that the premisses logically entail the conclusion, or that
the conclusion logically follows from the premisses.

As can be seen clearly, our definition (C29.6) of
normative validity can be applied equally well to (mixed)
normative arguments:

(29.8)   A₁, A₂, A₃, ..., A_k, , B₁, B₂, B₃, ..., B_m,   ∴ C

where each 'A_i' (i=1, 2, ..., k) and 'C' are normative
sentences (or, in particular, deontic sentences) and each 'B_j'
(j=1, 2, ..., m) is an assertoric sentence. We can likewise
say that a mixed normative argument (29.8) is valid if and
only if in every possible world the conclusion 'C' would be
true provided that the premisses 'A₁', 'A₂', ..., 'A_k', and 'B₁',
'B₂',..., 'B_m' should all be true.

Of course, the truth-value of 'A_i' is not determined
on the same basis on which we determine the truth-value
of 'B_j'. But this does not give us any trouble. All we want
to explicate in this case is: given a set of prescriptions
A₁, A₂, ..., A_k, and a set of propositions (assertions) B₁,

B_2, ..., B_m, whether or not the prescription C logically follows. Or, in other words, whether or not C is a logical consequence of the prescriptions A_1, A_2, ..., A_k together with the assertions B_1, B_2, ..., B_m. Here the difference in truth-basis between normative and assertoric premisses does not affect our explication.

The following (mixed) normative arguments will be judged valid according to our criterion of normative validity:

(29.9)   All and only logicians ought to teach logic.

John is a logician.

∴ John ought to teach logic.

(29.10)   Keep all your promises (if you have made any) !

This is one of your promises.

Keep it!

We regard (29.10) as an (imperative) argument equivalent to the following (deontic) one:

(29.10')   You ought to keep all your promises.

This is one of your promises.

You ought to keep it.

where we let 'You ought...' be a stylistic variant of 'It is obligatory that you...'

So far we have exhibited only normative arguments, pure or mixed, of a relatively simple type, namely, arguments of which the premisses and conclusions are all simple or "atomic" sentences. However, our validity criterion can readily be applied to the type of arguments in which some of the component sentences are compound or "molecular", multiplex or otherwise, because the truth value of these molecular sentences can be determined by the truth values of its component sentences together with definitions (D29.3). The following are some examples of arguments of this type.

All of them are valid.

(15.1)   Post the mail!
            Post the mail or burn it!

(29.11)   If it rains, close the window!
            You are permitted not to close the window.
            It does not rain.

(29.12)   Go fishing with John or stay at home studying
            logic!
            Do not go fishing with John!
            Stay at home studying logic!

These arguments, or more adequately speaking, the argument forms which these arguments instantiate, have received much attention in the literature. [5] Some philosophers, notably Ross and Williams among others, even use some of these examples to claim the implausibility of deontic logic and/or imperative logic. We shall come back to these arguments in § 32.

---

5 See, for example, Castañeda [1960b], Geach [1958], Keene [1966], Ross [1941] or [1944] and Williams [1963].

§ 30. SOUNDNESS OF NORMATIVE ARGUMENTS

In an equally straightforward way as we introduced the notion of normative validity, we may now introduce the notion of *normative soundness*.

(D30.1)   A normative argument is said to be *sound* if and only if, first of all, it is valid, and secondly, all its premises are true.

However, it should be noted that an argument may be sound with respect to one set of moral rules but unsound with respect to another set of moral rules, because the truth values of normative sentences are determined on the basis of a set of moral rules. For example, whether or not the following argument is sound depends upon what set of moral rules we use to determine the truth values of the premises.

> If you feel depressed, read Psalm 34!
> If you lose faith, read Psalm 37!
> Either you feel depressed or you lose faith.
> ∴ Read Psalm 34 or Psalm 37!

§ 31. SOME ADDITIONAL REMARKS ON THE EXPLICATION OF NORMATIVE VALIDITY

In § 28 we indicated that our concept of normative validity is proposed to explicate the notion of "logical following" applying to prescriptions. We want our criterion of normative validity to be able to decide whether or not a prescription logically follows from other prescriptions, i.e., to decide whether or not an evaluation logically follows from other evaluations, and to decide whether or not a command logically follows from other commands. Thus when we know that a normative argument

(28.1) $\quad A_1, A_2, A_3, ..., A_k, \quad \therefore C$

is valid, we know that

(31.1) The evaluation C is *necessarily* made (by a certain set of moral rules) provided that the evaluations $A_1, A_2, A_3, ..., A_k$ are all made (by that set of rules).

or

(31.2) The command C is *necessarily* issued (by a set of moral rules) provided that the commands $A_1, A_2, A_3, ..., A_k$ are all issued (by that set of rules).

Now, on the imperative side, our normative validity may be said to explicate another seemingly more significant intuitive notion. This notion can be explained as follows.

Suppose the argument (28.1) is valid, then (31.2)

above holds. But from (31.2) it follows that

(31.3) If one fulfills the commands A_1, A_2, A_3, ..., A_k, one *necessarily* fulfills the command C.

Hence,

(31.4) In order that one fulfills the commands A_1, A_2, A_3, ..., A_k, one *must* fulfill the command C.

Now, this notion of "must-fulfill-in-order-to-fulfill-A" may be called '*necessary fulfillment toward,* or *with respect to,* (the fulfillment of) A'[1]. Our concept of normative validity can then be thought of also as an explication of this notion.

For example, the following argument is valid:

(31.5) Keep all your promises!

∴ Keep your latest promise, if any!

the command

(31.6) Keep all your promises!

logically entails the following command:

(31.7) Keep your latest promise, if any!

Now, in order to fulfill the command (31.6), we *must* fulfill the command (31.7). Thus, we say that to bring about what is ordered in (31.7) is a necessary fulfillment toward the fulfillment of (31.6).

The notion of necessary fulfillment seems to be an important notion, and our theory of normative validity helps us to see whether to do something is a necessary fulfillment toward a certain command or certain commands.

However interesting the notion of necessary fulfillment

---

1 This is a relative notion. We may establish an absolute notion of necessary fulfillment, namely, the necessary fulfillment with respect to no commands. Commands which instantiate the following form are necessarily fulfilled by every one at any time in any place:

(!) p v~ (!) p

may be, it seems to be appropriately applicable only to orders of the following two forms: '(!) A' and '(X) A'. It is hard to say what state of affairs constitutes the fulfillment of the imperative '(#) A' or '(√) A'. Could this be one of the reasons why the latter two imperative operators are lacking in our natural language? But to ignore their existence or to confuse one of '(#) A' and '(√) A' with one of '(!) A' and '(X) A' may sometimes cause unnecessary misunderstanding in imperative logic as we shall see in the next section. [2]

At this point it may be pointed out that Leonard's definition of the truth value of an imperative can equally well be used to define our notion of normative validity, or in particular, *imperative validity*. According to Leonard, an imperative A is true or false according as A is fulfilled (by the recipient of the imperative) or not. [3] Now we may say, in accordance with our definition of normative validity, that a (pure) imperative argument

(28.1) $A_1, A_2, A_3, ..., A_k,$ $\therefore$ C

is valid if and only if it is impossible that $A_1, A_2, A_3, ...,$

---

[2] The most likely confusion is to mistake $\ulcorner \sim (!) A \urcorner$, that is $\ulcorner (√) \sim A \urcorner$ for $\ulcorner (X) A \urcorner$. The "negation" of 'Do!' is *not* 'Do not!' but rather the imperative counterpart of 'may not' or 'permitted not'.

[3] See Leonard [1959a]. What we stated is a simplification of his view. Leonard makes the following observations:

"An interesting aspect of imperatives is that although they express the will of the speaker, their truth or falsity depends upon the will of the addressee. The addressee may conform his will to that of the speaker and act in the manner indicated, or he may disregard the speaker's will and act in a contrary fashion. *According as he does the one or the other, he makes the imperative to be true or false.*" Ibid., p. 184, my italics.

A_k are all true, but C is false. This, according to Leonard, means that it is impossible that the imperatives A_1, A_2, A_3, ..., A_k are all fulfilled but the imperative C is not. This in turn says that if one fulfills the imperatives (commands) A_1, A_2, A_3, ..., A_k, one necessarily fulfills the imperative (command) C. But this is exactly what we have stated in (31.3) above. Thus, we see that although Leonard's definition of the truth value of an imperative is quite different from ours—the former is defined in terms of the fulfillment of the recipient of a command, the latter in terms of the moral rules which make the command—he might develop a notion of normative validity coincident with ours. This seems to indicate that Leonard's conception of the truth and falsehood of an imperative, and possibly also his view on the truth and falsehood of an interrogative because they are mutually related and are both based on a common ground in the theory of signs, although thus far not widely accepted, might prove to be an agreeable and workable one.

§ 32. UNDERSTANDING IMPERATIVE LOGIC

The study of imperatives and their relation with "assertorics" can be traced back at least as early as David Hume when he set himself to show, among other things, that "reason alone can never be a motive to any action of the will". [1] Early this century, Henri Poincaré made a similar but more cogent observation by proclaiming the impossibility of founding ethics on science. He argued that we can infer no moral sentences which are in the imperative mood from scientific sentences which are in the indicative mood. [2] These observations, while relevant and significant as they stand to imperative logic, are nevertheless at most vague and pre-systematic. It was the Danish philosopher Jørgen Jørgensen who in the 1930's attempted to "initiate a discussion on the logical character of imperatives". [3] He pointed out a "puzzle" in the imperative logic which is now commonly, but not quite adequately, called "Jørgensen's dilemma" [4] and thereby marked the era of modern discussion of imperative logic.

This dilemma, or puzzle as Jørgensen himself labeled

---

[1] Hume, *A Treatise of Human Nature*, Book II, section iii.

[2] Poincaré, "La morale et la science", *Dernières Pensées*, 1913, pp. 223—347.

[3] Jørgensen [1937], p. 288.

[4] See Jørgensen, *ibid.*, p. 290. The name 'Jørgensen's dilemma' was first used by Ross. See Ross [1944], p. 32.

it, may be reconstructed as follows. On the one hand, it seems that we are unable to construct a valid imperative argument or indeed any valid argument which consists of one or more imperative sentences. For validity is usually defined in terms of truth value. Thus, "according to a generally accepted definition of logical inference, only sentences which are capable of being true or false can function as premisses or conclusions in an inference".[5] But imperative sentences are neither true nor false. Hence, there can be no imperative arguments or mixed arguments with imperative premisses. Nevertheless, it seems, on the other hand, equally clear that there are arguments of the aforesaid sort of which the conclusion may be regarded as logically drawn from the premisses. For instance, the following one seems to be a perfectly good argument:

(29.10)   Keep all your promises!

This is one of your promises.

∴ Keep it!

It may be pointed out that the foregoing dilemma is not a genuine one, for the two horns taken together do not drive us with our back to the wall. The first half of the dilemma says that imperative logic is impossible on the "generally accepted" definition of validity, but the second half says that imperative logic seems possible—perhaps on a different notion of validity. We can avoid this dilemma simply by denying one or both of its two horns, asserting that imperative logic is possible and beginning to exploit the alternative notion of logical validity, namely, normative validity. Indeed, this is exactly what we have done in the

5 Jørgensen, ibid.

previous sections where we proclaimed that normative sentences, imperative ones in particular, are capable of being either true or false, and defined (normative) validity by means of the newly characterized truth value of sentences. [6]

It follows that to refute the possibility of imperative logic by saying that imperative sentences are incapable of being true or false, as the first horn of the Jørgensen's dilemma tries to do, is by no means convincing; neither is the reason conclusive. For one has also to show that assertoric validity is the only concept of validity acceptable to us. But this conviction is hardly tenable. For, otherwise, how can we have the inclination to say that normative arguments such as (29.10) are valid? They *could not* be, if the "generally accepted" definition of validity *were* the only sense of validity possibly acceptable to us!

There seems then to be no logical ground to rebut the possibility of imperative logic. However, some miscellaneous issues and questions have since been raised, and thereby certain misgivings and doubts expressed, in connection with imperative reasonings. [7] Since these misgivings are often taken as indications of the impossibility, or at least implausibility, of imperative logic, a close attention and careful examination of those issues and questions seems not only desirable but also crucial.

Let us examine these issues by going through some of

---

6 Our definition of validity set down in the previous sections aims primarily at deontic arguments. But we have indicated that it applies equally well to imperative arguments, since the latter are regarded as mirror copies of the former.

7 By an imperative reasoning or inference we mean a reasoning in which imperative sentences are involved.

the typical examples which we frequently find in the literature.

As we mentioned in § 15, Ross has given as an example of counter-intuitive imperative inference (or practical inference as it is sometimes called) the following one:

(15.1)   Post the letter!

        ∴ Post the letter or burn it!

Ross apparently realized that this argument could be regarded as valid in one sense. For he remarked that if the premiss has been satisfied, meaning that the letter has been slipped into the letter-box; then the conclusion, too, would have been satisfied, meaning similarly. [8] However, he commented immediately that"...it is equally obvious that this inference [namely, (15.1)] is not immediately *conceived* to be logically valid." [9] A similar point has also been advanced by B. A. O. Williams and G. B. Keene. [10] They, together with A. J. Kenny all, in one way or another, hold the view that "there is not in general anything that can be called *imperative inference*". [11]

To clarify the matter, let us first point out that (15.1) may be thought of as an imperative argument which instantiates either one of the following forms:

(32.1)   (!) p

        ∴ (!) p v (!) q

or

(32.2)   (!) p

---

8 Ross [1944], p. 38.

9 *Ibid.*, my italics.

10 See Williams [1963], pp. 31—32 and Keene [1966], pp. 57—63.

11 Williams, *ibid.*, p. 30, Keene, *ibid.*, p. 57, and Kenny [1966], p. 67.

$$\therefore \quad (!) \quad (p \lor q)$$

in which 'p' and 'q' stand, respectively, for 'Your mailing the letter' and 'Your burning the letter'. Now, the validity of (32.1) is justified by propositional logic, and the validity of (32.2) by (CMI$_R$T*23), namely,

(CMI$_R$T*23) $(!_R) \, p \supset (!_R) \, (p \lor q)$

Let us first argue for the validity of (15.1) by assuming that it has the form (32.1). What we claim to be valid then is the following argument:

(32.3)   Post the letter!

$\therefore$ (Post the letter!) v (Burn the letter!)

The meaning of the conclusion of (32.3) is perfectly clear from our definition (D29.2) — (D29.3), namely, 'v' is used here as the analogue of the wedge in propositional logic. That is, the conclusion of (32.3) commands either to post the letter, or to burn the letter or to do both. And as in the case of the truth-functional wedge, we read 'v' in (32.3) as 'or'. Hence, we have the valid argument (15.1).

Once we read the wedge in (32.2) as 'or', misunderstanding tends to creep in. In English the command

(32.4)   Post the letter or burn it!

when issued isolatedly, does convey the meaning that the addressee may choose either to post the letter or to burn it. In other words, (32.4), in that context, is equivalent to

(32.5) $[(!) \, p \lor (!) \, q] \, \& \, [(\surd) \, p \, \& \, (\surd) \, q]$

where 'p' and 'q' stand for the propositions we indicated above. This sense of 'or' is the same as, or at least equivalent to, what Åqvist calls the "choice-offering" 'or'. [12] However, it is obvious that we should not read this sense of 'or' into

12 See Åqvist [1965].

(32.3). It is fallacious, if not ridiculous, to think that from the command

(32.6)   Post the letter!

and the validity of (32.3) one can conclude that one may burn the letter. Nothing is farther from truth than this, for otherwise we could conclude anything at all!

To see the matter more clearly, let us first begin with the assertoric analogue of (15.1). We know that the following argument is valid:

$$2+4=6$$
$$\therefore \ 2+4=6 \text{ or } 4 \text{ and } 6 \text{ are relative primes.}$$

But from the truth of '2+4=6' and the validity of this argument, we do not jump to the conclusion that '4 and 6 are relative primes' is true. What, then, makes us become rapacious when we deal with similar imperative reasonings?

The reason seems to be this. Some people seem to believe that in order to fulfill a command we may simply fulfill *any* logical consequence of the command. Hence, in order to fulfill the command (32.6), one may simply fulfill its logical consequence (32.4). Now to interpret (32.4) as (32.5), one concludes, therefore, that in order to fulfill the command "post the letter!" one may simply go burn it.

The truth is that in order to fulfill a command one must fulfill *every* — *not* any — command which is a logical consequence of the original command. [13] (This includes, of course, the original command itself, because every command logically entails itself by a simple logical law, namely by the so-called "reflexive law of implication".) This follows

---

13 This point was brought to the author's attention by Professor Herbert E. Hendry.

from the fact, as we mentioned in the last section, that if A logicall entails B, then to bring about what B commands is a necessary fulfillment toward the fulfillment of A. Now, from (32.6), i.e., 'Post the letter!' $[(!)p]$ we can not only infer

(32.4)   Post the letter or burn it! $[(!)p \vee (!)q]$

but also

(32.7)   Post the letter or not-burn it [14] ! $[(!)p \vee (!) \sim q]$

Hence, we have to fulfill both (32.4) and (32.7), i.e. to fulfill

(32.8) $[(!)p \vee (!)q] \& [(!)p \vee (!) \sim q]$

But this, by PL, is equivalent to

(32.9) $(!)p \vee [(!)q \& (!) \sim q]$

However, it is commonly accepted, and indeed is a theorem, i.e., $(CMI_R T^*19)$, that

(32.10) $\sim [(!)q \& (!) \sim q]$

Consequently, by PL again, we conclude

(32.11) $(!)p$

That is to say, what we should do is to post the letter rather than do something else, in particular, we should not burn it!

Here we treated (15.1) as if it had the form (32.1). In case it has the form (32.2), similar argument can be put forth. This can be seen as follows. In order to fulfill (32.11), we have to fulfill

(32.12) $(!) (p \vee q)$

because we maintain that (32.2) is valid. Now, for the

---

14 We write 'not-burn it!' for '$\sim$ (burn it)' which, as we indicated above, is not equivalent to 'Do not burn it!' but rather to the imperative counterpart of 'you are permitted not to burn it'.

same reason, we must also fulfill

(32.13)   (!) (p v ~q)

Hence, we must fulfill

(32.14)   (!) (p v q) & (!) (p v ~q)

It follows that we must fulfill

(32.15)   (!) [(p v q) & (p v ~q)]

because

(32.16)   (!) (p v q) & (!) (p v ~q) ≡
                 (!) [(p v q) & (p v ~q)]

is an instance of a theorem, i.e., an instance of (CMI$_R$T*
27). But (32.15) is, by PL, equivalent to

(32.11)   (!) p

Again, what we should do is to post the mail, there is no
way to see that we may burn it.

Another question which has often been discussed in the
literature is whether or not the imperative counterpart of
modus tollens is a valid principle or valid argument form. [15]
The argument form in question is:

(32.17)   p ⊃ (!) q [16]

                ~ (!) q

             ∴ ~p

Casteñeda argues for the validity of *modus tollens,* but
he gives the following example:

(32.18)   If he comes, leave the files open!

             Do not leave the files open!

             ∴ He does not come.

This argument, valid or not, is not an instance of (32.17).
It instantiates another quite different argument form, namely.

---

15 See, for example, Casteñeda, *ibid.,* and Geach, *ibid.*

16 This argument form is valid according to our criterion.

(32.19) $p \supset (!) q$ [17]

$\qquad$ (X) q

$\qquad \therefore \sim p$

A further argument form which has received considerable attention is the imperative counterpart of the so-called disjunctive syllogism, [18] viz.,

(32.20) $(!) p \lor (!) q$

$\qquad \sim (!) q$

$\qquad \therefore (!) p$

or, in another form:

(32.21) $(!) (p \lor q)$

$\qquad (!) \sim q$

$\qquad \therefore (!) p$

It should be mentioned again that the negation of '(!) q' is '$(\checkmark) \sim q$' not '(X) q'. Hence, (32.20) is equivalent to

(32.22) $(!) p \lor (!) q$

$\qquad (\checkmark) \sim q$

$\qquad \therefore (!) p$

rather than to

(32.23) $(!) p \lor (!) q$

$\qquad (X) q$

$\qquad \therefore (!) p$

In giving examples, people tend to confuse (32.22) with (32.23). This seems a place to see the merit of bringing to our attention the two imperative operators which do not exist in English.

---

17 It is easy to see that (31.19) is a valid argument form. To show this, use $(CMI_R T*21)$. i.e.,

$\qquad \sim ((!) p \,\&\, (X) \sim p)$

and PL.

18 See, for example, Williams, *ibid.*

In concluding this section, let us mention, and it is easy to show, that all the argument forms (32.20) — (32.23) are valid.

APPENDICES

A. AXIOMS AND RULES

I. System vW*
   Axioms:
   - (A1) $\vdash p \supset [q \supset p]$
   - (A2) $\vdash [p \supset [q \supset r]] \supset [[p \supset q] \supset [p \supset r]]$
   - (A3) $\vdash [\sim q \supset \sim p] \supset [p \supset q]$
   - (Ad6) $\vdash P[p \lor q] \equiv . \; Pp \lor Pq$

   Rules:
   - (R1)   Substitution
   - (R2)   *modus ponens*
   - (Rd6) P-extensionality: From $\ulcorner A \equiv B \urcorner$ we may infer $\ulcorner PA \equiv PB \urcorner$.

II. System FÅ
   Axioms:
   - (FÅ1) $\vdash Oa \supset Pa$
   - (FÅ2) $\vdash Oa \& Ob . \supset OKab$
   - (FÅ3) $\vdash Pa \& Pb . \supset PKab$

   Rules:
   - (RFÅ1) Substitution
   - (RFÅ2) *modus ponens*
   - (RFÅ3) Extensionality: if $\ulcorner X \supset Y \urcorner$ is any of the PL-theorems PL1-PL8 listed below, and

$$X' = S \begin{array}{c} \text{'p', 'q', '} \sim \text{', '\&', 'v'} \\ \text{'a', 'b', 'N', 'K', 'A'} \end{array} X \Big|$$

   and

$$Y' = S \begin{array}{c} \text{'p', 'q', '} \sim \text{', '\&', 'v'} \\ \text{'a', 'b', 'N', 'K', 'A'} \end{array} Y \Big|$$

and the deontic connectives in X′ and Y′ are placed "correctly", then ⌜PX′⊃PY′⌝ is a theorem of FÅ.

(PL1)   ⊢ ~[p & q] ⊃ ~[q & p]

(PL2)   ⊢ [p & q] ⊃ p

(PL3)   ⊢ [p & q] ⊃ q

(PL4)   ⊢ [p & q] ⊃ [p v q]

(PL5)   ⊢ p ⊃ ~ ~ p

(PL6)   ⊢ ~ ~ p ⊃ p

(PL7)   ⊢ ~[~ ~p & ~ ~q] ⊃ ~[p & q]

(PL8)   ⊢ p ⊃ [p v q]

(RFA4) Replacement in PL-theorems: If X is any theorem of PL, and δ is a propositional variable, and C a deontic formula, then

$$S \overset{\delta}{\underset{C}{}} X \, \Big|$$

is a theorem of FÅ.

III. Systems OT*–OS5*

    Axioms:

  i) for OT*

    (A1) — (A3)   Same.

    (Ad4)   ⊢ O[p ⊃ q] ⊃ [Op ⊃ Oq]

    (Ad6)   ⊢ Op ⊃ ~O~p

    (Ad7)   ⊢ O[Op ⊃ p]

  ii) for OS4*

    Axioms for OT* plus (Ad8)

    (Ad8)   ⊢ Op ⊃ OOp

  iii) for OS5*

    Axioms fo OS4* plus (Ad9)

    (Ad9)   ⊢ ~Op ⊃ O~Op

  Rules (for OT*–OS5*):

(R1) – (R2)   Same

(Rd3)   Deontic necessitation: From A we may infer
⌜OA.⌝

IV. System OM-OM″

Axioms:

i) for OM

(A1) – (A3)   Same

(AN4)   ⊢ $p \supset \Diamond p$

(AN5)   ⊢ $\Diamond [p \vee q] \equiv [\Diamond p \vee \Diamond q]$

ii) for OM′

Axioms for OM plus (AN6)

(AN6)   ⊢ $\Diamond \Diamond p \supset \Diamond p$

iii) for OM″

Axioms for OM′ plus (AN7)

(AN7)   ⊢ $\Diamond \sim \Diamond p \supset \sim \Diamond p$

Rules (for OM–OM″) :

(R1) – (R2)   Same

(RN3)   Extensionality: From ⌜$A \supset B$⌝ we may infer
⌜$\Diamond A \supset \Diamond B.$⌝

(RN4)   Necessitation: From A we may infer
⌜$\sim \Diamond \sim A$⌝.

B. DEFINITIONS

System vW

  (D2.1) $\ulcorner O\alpha \urcorner =_{Df} \ulcorner \sim P \sim \alpha \urcorner$

  (D2.2) $\ulcorner F\alpha \urcorner =_{Df} \ulcorner \sim P\alpha \urcorner$

  (D2.3) $\ulcorner I\alpha \urcorner =_{Df} \ulcorner P\alpha \mathbin{\&} P \sim \alpha \urcorner$

Systems OT*-OS5*

  (Dd1) $\ulcorner PA \urcorner =_{Df} \ulcorner \sim O \sim A \urcorner$

  (Dd2) $\ulcorner FA \urcorner =_{Df} \ulcorner \sim PA \urcorner$

  (Dd3) $\ulcorner IA \urcorner =_{Df} \ulcorner PA \mathbin{\&} P \sim A \urcorner$

Systems OM-OM″

  (DN1) $\ulcorner \Box A \urcorner =_{Df} \ulcorner \sim \Diamond \sim A \urcorner$

  (DN2) $\ulcorner A \rightarrow3 B \urcorner =_{Df} \ulcorner \Box [A \supset B] \urcorner$

  (DN3) $\mathscr{S} =_{Df}$ '$\mathscr{B} \mathbin{\&} \Diamond \sim \mathscr{B}$'

  (DN4) $\ulcorner PA \urcorner =_{Df} \ulcorner \Diamond [A \mathbin{\&} \sim \mathscr{S}] \urcorner$

  (DN5) $\ulcorner FA \urcorner =_{Df} \ulcorner \sim PA \urcorner$

  (DN7) $\ulcorner IA \urcorner =_{Df} \ulcorner PA \mathbin{\&} P \sim A \urcorner$

Systems $\mathrm{CMO_R T^*}$-$\mathrm{CMO_R S5^*}$

  (D17.1) $\ulcorner O_R A^* \urcorner =_{Df}$ R requires that A*.

  (D17.2) $\ulcorner P_R A^* \urcorner =_{Df} \ulcorner \sim O_R \sim A^* \urcorner$

  (D17.3) $\ulcorner F_R A^* \urcorner =_{Df} \ulcorner \sim P_R A^* \urcorner$

  (D17.4) $\ulcorner I_R A^* \urcorner =_{Df} \ulcorner P_R A^* \mathbin{\&} P_R \sim A^* \urcorner$

Systems $\mathrm{CMI_R T^*}$-$\mathrm{CMI_R S5^*}$

  (D25.3) $\ulcorner (!_R) A^* \urcorner =_{Df}$ R requires that A*.

  (D24.1) $\ulcorner (\surd_R) A^* \urcorner =_{Df} \ulcorner \sim (!_R) \sim A^* \urcorner$

  (D24.2) $\ulcorner (X_R) A^* \urcorner =_{Df} \ulcorner \sim (\surd_R) A^* \urcorner$

  (D24.3) $\ulcorner (\#_R) A^* \urcorner =_{Df} \ulcorner (\surd_R) A^* \mathbin{\&} (\surd_R) \sim A^* \urcorner$

C. THEOREMS (OT*–OS5*)

(OT*1)	$\vdash Op \equiv \sim P \sim p$
(OT*2)	$\vdash Op \equiv F \sim p$
(OT*3)	$\vdash Pp \equiv \sim Fp$
(OT*4)	$\vdash Pp \equiv \sim O \sim p$
(OT*5)	$\vdash Fp \equiv \sim Pp$
(OT*6)	$\vdash Fp \equiv O \sim p$
(OT*7)	$\vdash O \sim p \equiv \sim Pp$
(OT*8)	$\vdash P \sim p \equiv \sim Op$
(OT*9)	$\vdash F \sim p \equiv \sim P \sim p$
(OT*10)	$\vdash Ip \equiv Pp \,\&\, P \sim p$
(OT*11)	$\vdash OP \supset Pp$
(OT*12)	$\vdash O \sim p \supset \sim Op$
(OT*13)	$\vdash \sim Pp \supset P \sim p$
(OT*14)	$\vdash Fp \supset \sim Op$
(OT*15)	$\vdash Fp \supset \sim F \sim p$
(OT*16)	$\vdash F \sim p \supset Pp$
(OT*17)	$\vdash O \,(p \, v \sim p)$
(OT*18)	$\vdash F \,(p \, \& \sim p)$
(OT*19)	$\vdash \sim (Op \,\&\, O \sim p)$
(OT*20)	$\vdash Pp \, v \, P \sim p$
(OT*21)	$\vdash \sim (Op \,\&\, Fp)$
(OT*22)	$\vdash O \,(p \, \& \sim p) \supset Oq$
(OT*23)	$\vdash Op \supset O \,(p \, v \, q)$
(OT*24)	$\vdash Pp \supset P \,(p \, v \, q)$
(OT*25)	$\vdash Fp \supset F \,(p \,\&\, q)$
(OT*26)	$\vdash F \,(p \, v \, q) \supset Fp$

(OT*27) $\vdash O\,(p\,\&\,q) \equiv .\ Op\,\&\,Oq$

(OT*28) $\vdash P\,(p\,v\,q) \equiv .\ Pp\,v\,Pq$

(OT*29) $\vdash F\,(p\,v\,q) \equiv .\ Fp\,\&\,Fq$

(OT*30) $\vdash O\,(p\,v\,q) \supset .\ Pp\,v\,Pq$

(OT*31) $\vdash P\,(p\,\&\,q) \supset .\ Pp\,\&\,Pq$

(OT*32) $\vdash Op\,v\,Oq. \supset O\,(p\,v\,q)$

(OT*33) $\vdash Fp \supset O\,(p \supset q)$

(OT*34) $\vdash Oq \supset O\,(p \supset q)$

(OT*35) $\vdash Op\,\&\,O\,(p \supset q)\ .\ \supset Oq$

(OT*36) $\vdash Pp\,\&\,O\,(p \supset q)\ .\ \supset Pq$

(OT*37) $\vdash Fq\,\&\,O\,(p \supset q)\ .\ \supset Fp$

(OT*38) $\vdash (Fq\,\&\,Fr)\,\&\,O\,(p \supset (q\,v\,r))\ .\ \supset Fp$

(OT*39) $\vdash \sim (O\,(p\,v\,q)\,\&\,(Fp\,\&\,Fq))$

(OT*40) $\vdash Op\,\&\,O\,((p\,\&\,q) \supset r)\ .\ \supset O\,(q \supset r)$

(OT*41) $\vdash Fp\,\&\,Fq\ .\ \supset F\,(p\,\&\,q)$

(OT*42) $\vdash Fp\,\&\,Oq\ .\ \supset F\,(p\,\&\,q)$

(OT*43) $\vdash Fp\,\&\,Ip\ .\ \supset F\,(p\,\&\,q)$

(OT*44) $\vdash Fp\,v\,Op\,v\,Ip$

(OT*45) $\vdash Ip \supset I \sim p$

(OT*46) $\vdash OOp \supset Op$

(OT*47) $\vdash OFp \supset Fp$

(OT*48) $\vdash FPp \supset Fp$

(OT*49) $\vdash FP \sim p \supset Op$

(OT*50) $\vdash O\,(Fp \supset \sim p)$

(OT*51) $\vdash O\,(p \supset Pp)$

(OT*52) $\vdash Op \supset OPp$

(OT*53) $\vdash Fp \supset FOp$

(OT*54) $\vdash PFp \supset P \sim p$

(OT*55) $\vdash POp \supset Pp$

(OT*56) $\vdash Pp \supset PPp$

(OS4*57) $\vdash O \sim p \supset OO \sim p$

(OS4*58) $\vdash O \sim p \equiv OO \sim p$

(OS4*59) $\vdash PPp \equiv Pp$

(OS4*60) $\vdash OOp \equiv Op$

(OS4*61) $\vdash O \sim Op \supset \sim Op$

(OS4*62) $\vdash O \sim Op \equiv O \sim O \sim O \sim Op$

(OS5*63) $\vdash O \sim Op \equiv \sim Op$

BIBLIOGRAPHY

I) A General Bibliography of Deontic Logic and Imperative Logic

This bibliography includes most of the important works in deontic logic and imperative logic published before 1968. However, only those publications appearing in English are listed except in some cases we give non-English titles for completeness.

The starred items are explicitly mentioned or referred to in this discussion.

Allen, L.E.

(1960)   "Deontic Logic", *Modern Uses of Logic in Law*, vol. 60, pp. 13-27.

Anderson, A.R.

* (1956)   *The Formal Analysis of Normative Systems*, A Technical Report to the Office of Naval Research, Yale University.

(1958a)   "The Logic of Norms", *Logique et Analyse*, vol. 1, pp. 84-91.

(1958b)   "A Reduction of Deontic Logic to Alethic Modal Logic", *Mind*, vol. 67, pp. 100-103.

(1959)   "On the Logic of 'Commitment'", *Phil. Studies*, vol. 10, pp. 23-27.

(1962)   "Reply to Mr. Rescher", *Phil. Studies*, vol. 13, pp. 6-8.

(1967)   "Some Nasty Problems in the Formal Logic of Ethics", *Noûs*, vol. 1, pp. 345-360.

Anderson, A.R. and O.K. Moore
(1957)   "The Formal Analysis of Normative Concepts", *The American Sociological Review*, vol. 22, pp. 9-17.

Apostel, L.
(1960)   "Game Theory and the Interpretation of Deontic Logic", *Logique et Analyse*, vol. 3, pp. 70-90.

Bar-Hillel, Y.
(1966)   "Imperative Inference", *Analysis*, vol. 26, pp. 79-82.

Beardsley, E.L.
(1944)   "Imperative Sentences in Relation to Indicatives", *The Phil. Review*, vol. 53, pp. 175-185.

Berg, J.
(1960)   "A Note on Deontic Logic", *Mind*, vol. 69, pp. 566-567.

Bergström, L.
(1962)   *Imperatives and Ethics*, Filosofiska studier utgivna av Filosofiska Institutionen vid Stockholms Universitet, Stockholm.

Beth, E.W.
(1946-47) "Discussion", *Synthese*, vol. 5, pp. 94-95.

Bohnert, H.G.
*(1945)   "The Semiotic Status of Commands", *Phil. of Science*, vol. 12, pp. 302-315.

Castañeda, H.N.

(1955)   "A Note on Imperative Logic", *Phil. Studies,* vol. 6, pp. 1-4.

(1957)   "On the Logic of Norms", *Methodos,* vol. 9, pp. 209-215.

(1958)   "Imperatives and Deontic Logic", *Analysis,* vol. 19, pp. 42-48.

(1959)   "The Logic of Obligation", *Phil. Studies,* vol. 10, pp. 17-22.

(1960a)   "Obligation and Modal Logic", *Logique et Analyse,* vol. 3, pp. 40—48.

*(1960b) "Imperative Reasonings", *Phil. and Phenom. Research,* vol. 21, pp. 21-49.

(1964)   "Correction to "The Logic of Obligation" (A Reply)", *Phil. Studies,* vol. 15, pp. 25-28.

(1966)   "A Note on Deontic Logic (A Rejoinder)", *The Journal of Phil.,* vol. 63, pp. 231-234.

(1967a)   "Actions, Imperative, and Obligations", *Aristotelian Society,* 2797, pp. 25-48.

(1967b)   "Indicators and Quasi-Indicators", *Am. Phil. Quart.,* vol. 4, pp. 85-100.

(1968)   "Acts, the Logic of Obligation, and Deontic Calculi", *Phil. Studies,* vol. 19, pp. 13-26.

Castañeda, H.N. and G. Nakhnikian

(1962)   See Nakhnikian.

Chisholm, R.M.

*(1963a) "Contrary-to-duty Imperatives and Deontic Logic", *Analysis,* vol. 24, pp. 33-36.

*(1963b) "Supererogation and Offence", *Ratio,* vol. 5, pp. 1-14.

    (1964)   "The Ethics of Requirement", *Am. Phil. Quart.*, vol. 1, pp. 147-153.

Cohen, J.
    (1951)   "Three-Valued Ethics", *Philosophy*, vol, 26, pp. 208-227.

Cresswell, M.J.
    (1967)   "Some Further Semantics for Deontic Logic", *Logique et Analyse*, vol. 10, pp. 179-191.

Davidson, D.
    (1967)   "The Logical Form of Action Sentences", In Rescher (1967a), pp. 81-95.

Dawson, E.E.
    (1959)   "A Model for Deontic Logic", *Analysis,* vol. 19, pp. 73-78.

Downing, P.B.
    (1961)   "Opposite Conditionals and Deontic Logic", *Mind,* vol. 70, pp. 491-502.

Espersen, J.
  * (1967)   "The Logic of Imperatives", *Danish Yearbook of Phil.,* vol. 4, pp. 57-112.

Fenstad, J.E.
    (1959a)   "Notes on Normative Logic", *Avhandlinger utgitt av Det Norske Videnskaps-Akademi i Oslo,* Oslo.
    (1959b)   "Notes on the Application of Formal Methods in the Soft Sciences", *Inquiry,* vol. 2, pp. 34-64.

Fisher, M.
    (1961a)   "A Logical Theory of Commanding", *Logique*

et Analyse, vol. 4, pp. 154-169.

* (1961b) "A Three-Valued Calculus for Deontic Logic", *Theoria*, vol. 27, pp. 107-118.

(1962a) "On a so-called Paradox of Obligation", *The Journal of Phil.*, vol. 59, pp. 23-26.

(1962b) "Strong and Weak Negation of Imperatives", *Theoria*, vol. 28, pp. 196-200.

(1962c) "A System of Deontic-Alethic Modal Logic", *Mind*, vol. 71, pp. 231-236.

(1965) "A Contradiction in Deontic Logic?", *Analysis*, vol. 25, pp. 12-13.

Fitch, F.B.

(1963) "A Logical Analysis of Some Value Concepts", *The Journal of Sym. Logic*, vol. 28, pp. 135-142.

* (1966) "Natural Deduction Rules for Obligation", *Am. Phil. Quart.*, vol. 3. pp. 27-38.

Geach, P.T.

(1958) "Imperative and Deontic Logic" *Analysis*, vol. 18, pp. 49-56.

* (1963) "Imperative Inference", *Analysis*, vol. 23 (Suppl.), pp. 37-42.

(1966) "Dr. Kenny on Practical Inference", *Analysis*, vol. 26, pp. 76-79.

Gibbons, P.C.

(1960) "Imperatives and Indicatives", *Australasian Journal of Phil.*, vol. 38, pp. 107-119 and 207-219.

Goble, L.F.

* (1966) "The Iteration of Deontic Modalities", *Logique*

et Analyse, vol. 9, pp. 197-209.

Grelling, K.
* (1939) "Zur Logik der Sollsätze", *Unity of Science Forum*, pp. 44-47.

Hanson, W.H.
* (1965) "Semantics for Deontic Logic", *Logique et Analyse*, vol. 8, pp. 177-190.
(1966) "A Logic of Commands", *Logique et Analyse*, vol. 9, pp. 318-329.

Hare, R.M.
(1949) "Imperatives Sentences", *Mind*, vol. 58, pp. 21-39.
(1961) *The Language of Morals*, Oxford.
(1967) "Some Alleged Differences between Imperatives and Indicatives", *Mind*, vol. 76, pp. 309-326.

Hintikka, J.J.K.
* (1957) "Quantifiers in Deontic Logic", *Societas Scientiarum Fennica, Commontationes humanarum letterarum*, Helsingfors, vol. 23, p. 1023.

Hofstadter, A. and J. C. C. McKinsey
* (1939) "On the Logic of Imperative", *Phil. of Science*, vol. 6, pp. 446-457.

Holmes, R.L.
(1967) "Negation and the Logic of Deontic Assertions", *Inquiry*, vol. 10, pp. 89-95.

Jarvis, J.
(1962) "Practical Reasoning", *Phil. Quart.*, vol. 12, pp. 316-328.

Jørgensen, J.
* (1937)   "Imperatives and Logic", *Erkenntnis*, vol. 7, pp. 288-296.
  (1938)   "Imperatives og Logik" ("Imperative and Logic"), *Theoria*, vol. 4, pp. 183-190.

Keene, G.B.
* (1966)   "Can Commands Have Logical Consequences?", *Am. Phil. Quart.*, vol. 3, pp. 57-63.

Kenny, A.J.
* (1966)   "Practical Inference", *Analysis*, vol. 26, pp. 65-75.

Lemmon, E.J.
  (1960)   See Nowell-Smith.
  (1962)   "Moral Dilemmas", *Phil. Review*, vol. 71, pp. 139-158.
  (1965)   "Deontic Logic and the Logic of Imperatives", *Logique et Analyse*, vol. 8, pp. 39-71

McKinsey, J.C.C.
  (1939)   See Hofstadter.

McLaughlin. R. N.
  (1955)   "Further Problems of Derived Obligation". *Mind* vol. 64, pp. 400-402.

Mally, E.
* (1926)   *Grundgesetze des Sollens: Elemente der Logic des Willens*, Graz.

Marcus, R.B.
* (1966)   "Iterated Deontic Modalities", *Mind*, vol. 75, pp. 580-582.

Menger, K.

* (1939)   "A Logic of the Doubtful. On Optative and Imperative Logic", *Reports of a Mathematical Colloquium*, Univ. of Notre Dame, pp. 53-64.

Meredith, D.

(1956)   "A Correction to von Wright's Decision Procedure for the Deontic System P", *Mind*, vol. 65, pp. 548-550.

Moore, O.K.

(1957)   See Anderson.

Nakhnikian. G. and H. N. Castañeda (eds.)

(1962)   *Morality and the Language of Conduct*, Detroit.

Nowell-Smith, P. H. and E.J. Lemmon

(1960)   "Escapism: The Logical Basis of Ethics", *Mind*, vol. 69, pp. 289-300.

Nozick, R. and R. Routley

(1962)   "Escaping the Good Samaritan Paradox", *Mind*, vol. 71, pp. 377-382.

Peters, A.F.

(1949)   "R. M. Hare on Imperative Sentences: A Criticism", *Mind*, vol. 58, pp. 535-540.

Prior, A.N.

* (1954)   "The Paradoxes of Derived Obligation", *Mind*, vol. 63, pp. 64-65.

* (1956)   "A Note on the Logic of Obligation", *Revue Philosophique de Louvain*, vol. 54, pp. 86-87.

(1957)   *Time and Modality*, Oxford.

(1958)   "Escapism: The Logical Basis of Ethics", in Melden, A.I. (Ed.) *Essays in Moral Philos-*

ophy, Seattle, pp. 135-146.

*(1962)   *Formal Logic*, Second ed., Oxford.

(1964)   "The Done Thing". *Mind*, vol. 73, pp. 441-442.

(1967)   "Logic, Deontic", *The Encyclopedia of Philosophy* (ed.) P. Edwards, New York, pp. 509-513.

Rand, R.

(1962)   "The Logic of Demand-Sentence", *Syntheses*, vol 14,. pp. 237-254.

Rescher, N.

*(1958)   "An Axiom System for Deontic Logic", *Phil. Studies*, vol. 9, pp. 24-30 (A Corrigenda on p. 64)

*(1962)   "Conditional Permission in Deontic Logic", *Phil. Studies*, vol. 13, pp. 1-6.

(1964)   "Can One Infer Commands from Commands?", *Analysis*, vol. 24, pp. 176-179.

(1966a)   *Logic of Commands*, New York.

(1966b)   "Recent Trends and Developments in Logic", *Logique et Analyse*, vol. 9, pp. 269-279.

*(1967a)   *The Logic of Decision and Action* (ed.), Pittsburgh.

(1967b)   "Aspects of Action", in Rescher (1967a), pp. 215-219.

Rickman, H.P.

(1963)   "Escapism: The Logical Basis of Ethics", *Mind*, vol. 72, pp. 273-274.

Robison, J.

(1964)   "Who, What, Where, and When: A Note

on Deontic Logic", *Phil. Studies*, vol. 15, pp. 89-92.

Routley, R.
  (1962) See Nozick.

Ross, A.
  * (1941) "Imperative and Logic", *Theoria*, vol. 7, pp. 53-72.
  * (1944) "Imperatives and Logic", *Phil. of Science*, vol. 11, pp. 30-46, (Reprint of (1941)).
  (1964) "On Moral Reasoning", *Danish Yearbook of Phil.*, vol. 1, pp. 120-132.
  * (1966) *Directives and Norms*, London

Sellars, W.
  (1956) "Imperatives, Intentions and the Logic of 'Ought'", *Methodos*, vol. 8, pp. 227-268.

Sluya, H.D.
  (1963) "Some Remarks on Deontics", *Theoria*, vol. 29, pp. 70-78.

Smiley, T.J.
  (1963a) "Relative Necessity", *The Journal of Sym. Logic*, vol. 28, pp. 113-134.
  (1963b) "The Logical Basis of Ethics", *Acta Philosophica Fennica*, vol. 16, pp. 237-246.

Sosa, E.
  (1965) "Actions and Their Results", *Logique et Analyse*, vol. 8, pp. 111-125.
  (1966a) "The Logic of Imperatives", *Theoria*, vol. 32, pp. 224-235.
  (1966b) "On Practical Inference and the Logic of Imperatives", *Theoria*, vol. 32, pp. 211-223.

(1966c)   "Imperative and Referential Opacity", *Analysis*, vol. 27, pp. 49-52.

(1967)   "The Semantics of Imperatives", *Am. Phil. Quart.*, vol. 4, pp. 57-64.

Stenius, E.

(1963)   "The Principles of a Logic of Normative Systems", *Acta Philosophica Fennica*, vol. 16, pp. 247-260.

Williams, S.A.O.

* (1963)   "Imperative Inference", *Analysis*, vol. 23 (Suppl.), pp. 30-36.

Wright, G.H. von

* (1951a)   "Deontic Logic", *Mind*, vol. 60, pp. 1-15.

* (1951b)   *An Essay in Modal Logic*, Amsterdam.

(1952)   "On the Logic of Some Axiological and Epistemological Concepts", *Ajatus*, vol. 17, pp. 213-234.

(1955)   "Om s. k. praktiska slutledningar", *Tidsskrift for Rettsvitenskap*, vol. 68, pp. 465-495.

* (1956)   "A Note on Deontic Logic and Derived Obligation", *Mind*, vol. 65, pp. 507-509.

(1957)   *Logical Studies*, New York

(1963a)   *The Logic of Preference*, Edinburgh.

* (1963b)   *Norm and Action*, London.

(1963c)   *The Varieties of Goodness*, London.

* (1964)   "A New System of Deontic Logic", *The Danish Yearbook of Phil.*, vol. 1, pp. 173-182.

* (1965a)   "A Correction to a New System of Deontic Logic", *The Danish Yearbook of Phil.*, vol. 2, pp. 103-107.

* (1965b) ""And Next"", *Acta Philosophica Fennica,* vol. 18, pp. 293-304.

* (1966) ""And Then"", *Societas Scientiarum Fennica, Commentationes Physico-Mathematicae,* vol. 32, pp. 1-11.

(1967a) "Deontic Logic", *Am. Phil. Quart.,* vol. 4, pp. 136-143.

(1967b) "The Logic of Action—A Sketch", in Rescher (1967a), pp. 121-139.

Åqvist, L.

(1962a) "Interpretations of Deontic Logic", *Filosofiska Studier tillägnade Konrad Marc-Wogau den 4 April 1962,* Uppsala, pp. 15-23.

(1962b) "A Binary Primitive in Deontic Logic", *Logique et Analyse,* vol. 5, pp. 90-97.

(1963a) "A Note on Commitment", *Phil. Studies,* vol. 14, pp. 22-25.

* (1963b) "Postulate Sets and Decision Procedures for Some Systems of Deontic Logic", *Theoria,* vol. 29. pp 154-175.

* (1963c) "Deontic Logic Based on a Logic of 'Better'", *Acta Philosophica Fennica,* vol. 16, pp. 285-290.

(1964a) "On Dawson-models for Deontic Logic", *Logique et Analyse,* vol. 7, pp. 14-21.

(1964b) "Interpretations of Deontic Logic", *Mind,* vol. 73, pp. 246-253.

* (1965) "Choice-offering and Alternative-presenting Disjunctive Commands", *Analysis,* vol. 25, pp. 185-187.

* (1966) ""Next" and "Ought"", *Logique et Analyse,*

vol. 34, pp. 231-251.

*(1967)   "Good Samaritans, Contrary-to-Duty Imper-
atives, and Epistemic Obligations", *Noûs*, vol.
1, no. 4, pp. 361-379.

II) Other References

Church, A.
(1956)   *Introduction to Mathematical Logic,* vol. I,
Princeton.

Feys, R.
(1937-38)   "Les logiques nouvelles des modalités",
Revue Néoscholastique de Philosophie, vol.
40, pp. 517-553, and vol. 41, pp. 217-252.
(1955)   "Expression modale du 'devoir-être'", *Journal
of Sym. Logic,* vol. 20, pp. 91-92.
(1956)   "Reply to A. N. Prior 'A Note on the Logic
of Obligation'", *Revue Philosophique de
Louvain,* vol. 54, pp. 88-89.
(1965)   *Modal Logics,* Louvain and Paris.

Halldén, S.
(1957)   *The Logic of Better,* Copenhagen.

Hintikka, J.   "The Modes of Modality", *Acta Philosophica
Fennica,* vol. 16, pp. 65-81.

Kripke, S.A.
(1963)   "Semantical Analysis of Modal Logic (1),
Normal Modal Propositional Calculi", *Zeits-
chrift für Mathematische Logik und*

Grundlagen der Mathematik, vol. 9, pp. 67-96.

Leonard, H.S.
(1957) *Principls of Right Reason*, New York.
(1959a) "Interrogatives, Imperatives, Truth, Falsity and Lies", *Phil. of Science*, vol. 26, pp. 172-186.
(1959b) "Authorship and Purpose", *Phil. of Science*, vol. 26, pp. 277-294.
(1961) "A Reply to Professor Wheatley", *Phil. of Science*, vol. 28, pp. 55-64.
(1967) *Principles of Reasoning*, New York.

Łukasiewicz, J. and A. Tarski
(1930) "Untersuchungen über den Aussagenkalkül", *Sprawozdania z posiedzeń Towarzystwa Naukowego Warszawskiego*, vol. 23, no. 1-3 (in *Comptes rendus des séances de la Société des Sciences et des lettres de Varsovie*, Classe III) pp. 30-50.

Massey, G.J.
(1969) *Understanding Symbolic Logic*, New York.

Quine, W.V.O.
(1950) *Methods of Logic*, New York. (Rev. ed., 1959)

Sobociński, B.
(1953) "Note on a Modal System of Feys-von Wright", *Journal of Computing Systems*, vol. 1. pp. 171-178.

Tarski, A.
(1930) See Łukasiewicz.

三民大學用書 (一)

書　　　名	著作人	任　教　學　校
中 國 哲 學 史	周世輔	政　治　大　學
西 洋 哲 學 史	傅偉勳	臺　灣　大　學
邏　　　輯	林正弘	臺　灣　大　學
中 國 通 史	林瑞翰	臺　灣　大　學
中 國 法 制 史	戴炎輝	臺　灣　大　學
中國政治制度史	張金鑑	政　治　大　學
中國政治思想史	薩孟武	臺　灣　大　學
西洋政治思想史	張金鑑	政　治　大　學
國 父 思 想	周世輔	政　治　大　學
中華民國憲法論	管 歐	東　吳　大　學
比 較 憲 法	鄒文海	政　治　大　學
歐洲各國政府	張金鑑	政　治　大　學
美 國 政 府	張金鑑	政　治　大　學
政　治　學	曹伯森	陸　軍　官　校
行　政　學	左潞生	中　興　大　學
法 學 緒 論	鄭玉波	臺　灣　大　學
刑 法 總 論	蔡墩銘	臺　灣　大　學
刑 法 各 論	蔡墩銘	臺　灣　大　學
刑事訴訟法論	胡開誠	臺　灣　大　學

三民大學用書 (二)

書　　　名	著作人	任　教　學　校
監　　獄　　學	林紀東	臺　灣　大　學
民　法　總　則	鄭玉波	臺　灣　大　學
民法債編總論	鄭玉波	臺　灣　大　學
民　法　物　權	鄭玉波	臺　灣　大　學
民　法　親　屬	陳棋炎	臺　灣　大　學
民　法　繼　承	陳棋炎	臺　灣　大　學
公　　司　　法	鄭玉波	臺　灣　大　學
票　　據　　法	鄭玉波	臺　灣　大　學
海　　商　　法	鄭玉波	臺　灣　大　學
保　險　法　論	鄭玉波	臺　灣　大　學
保　　險　　法	袁宗蔚	政　治　大　學
社　會　思　想　史	龍冠海	臺　灣　大　學
社　　會　　學	龍冠海	臺　灣　大　學
勞　工　問　題	陳國鈞	中　興　大　學
社　會　立　法	劉修如 陳國鈞	臺中　灣興　大大　學學
現代企業管理	龔平邦	成　功　大　學
會　　計　　學	蔣友文	臺　灣　大　學
銀　行　會　計	李兆萱 金桐林	臺灣　政治　大大　學學
政　府　會　計	李增榮	政　治　大　學